# Unraveling

*A Collection in Poem and
Personal Perception*

# GARY G. SCOTT

ISBN 978-1-63844-356-8 (paperback)
ISBN 978-1-63844-357-5 (digital)

Christian Faith Publishing, Inc.
832 Park Avenue
Meadville, PA 16335
www.christianfaithpublishing.com

Printed in the United States of America

# Unraveling

A Collection by Gary G. Scott

Life begins like a tightly wound ball of yarn. What is loved, what is despised—accomplishments, disappointments, sorrows, and joys—begin falling upon that ancient floor of passing time. Eons will likely continue. Humankind will constantly progress, both for good and for bad. Time will maintain its assigned march, if God permits. And memories of individuals and their deeds will eventually be lost and forever forgotten.

*Unravel* has 2 meanings. 1, to bring out of a tangled state, to work out the problems of, to investigate, to solve, to begin to fail or collapse—*his life started to completely unravel.* 2, to undo or become undone, to separate the threads or strands of, to unwind, to pull apart—*the old sweater is unraveling.*

For my *unraveling*, meaning number 2 is being used. The moment of life (and only God knows when that moment is) this yarn begins to rapidly unwind. It methodically becomes undone, separating and pulling apart in total disregard of the time that's been given.

And every person has a vault filled with unraveling yarn. An abridgment, a snapshot, a collection of the fabric that makes you who you are and me who I am. As this yarn, this life, relentlessly unwinds. No one can command it to be stopped or slowed or hurried along. It is more treasured than all of earth's riches yet cannot be sold or bartered away. It's the home of a living soul; a soul that would never be exchanged for anything else *(Matthew 16:26).* Its value is beyond measure, containing the precious, unique particles that fashion each of us into a distinct person.

A soul of such value should receive great love and care. After all, we each have but one life, and there will be but one judgment of that life *(Hebrews 9:27)*. With this, in the early part of the 21$^{st}$ century, there are approximately 8 billion living souls—8 billion balls of unraveling yarn. Yet only God knows of the countless numbers that have already been or indeed of those still to come.

Eventually, mine will also rest on that ancient floor. But just as a single photograph cannot show the whole of any one life, so too is this collection. A simple snapshot of some of the things I love and some that I loathe. An abbreviated arrangement of principles and convictions. A snapshot lacking detail and yet retaining a fleeting image of what time will still inevitably take back. The unraveled remnants of yet another ball of yarn.

*On the final pages, you'll find "That Is to Say." Like a book with answers in the back, these "answers" are only what I had in mind. You can use them or lose them. Sometimes a thought can be written down but then its meaning forgotten. Admittedly, this happens. And so to avoid the consequences of memory lapse, "That Is to Say" has been added.*

# Chapter 1

## Time

But nothing on this earth can stop the process of this yarn unraveling. Time is like the pyroclastic flow of a volcano moving violently and swiftly, taking everything and everyone in its path. Although it moves consistently (the ticking of a clock), our perception will sometimes vary and oftentimes seem quite erratic—but it's not. We simply must accept the little piece that we've been given and hopefully fashion it to be acceptable and pleasing to God.

Time proceeds continually without favoritism. No given moment is any higher or any lower than any other. Kind of like how we are in God's sight—everyone is equal. So no one should vault themselves above others. For just as no second or minute or hour is of more value or importance than another, neither is any one person more valuable than any other.

# 2:27 AM

Why did he come rapping my door?
Disturbing my sleep,
Awakening me on his early morn round,
Taking back what no mortal can keep.

Quite politely, I asked him to stay…but he wouldn't.
He thought of himself something special…he shouldn't.
For his presence soon passed.
Not one second could wait.
Not one moment adorned as a King.
So I bade him farewell,
Dozing off back to sleep.
And the clock down the hall fell to 2:28.

September 23, 2008

(The only thing that makes time special is how you use it.)

But a second, a minute, indeed a year passes oh so quickly. As does even a long life. As James said in *James 4:14*, an entire lifetime is like a vapor that quickly vanishes away. Each tick of the clock lingers but only so very briefly for each and every one.

# Along the Coursing Tide

Uncountable, her bellows doeth the sea contain.
That stir within her depths from now through eons past.
That come, then fall upon some distant shore.
Or harbor find as ages press by islands yet unformed.

I stand beside that tide's expanse
And watch a single wave selected from the throng.
Rising high, it scours the wind
Only to disperse on earth and sand.
For it, as I,
A speck of passing time,
A carefully scripted symphony
Rehearsed and played...
Must end.

2005

# Tick

He latched upon me quickly
As I drew my waking breath.
And, keeping vigil, clung thereon;
Walked with me every step.

Often I would dine with him
Or his presence there neglect.
My friend at times…my enemy…
My comrade…my antagonist.

In staunch allegiance rolls his drum
Collecting every host.
No living dare to stand against his mighty armament
But trudges on in apathy.
The gleaner plucking from the vine
All those who entertain his mesmerizing dance.

Such fruit cannot be sweetened more,
Nor pressed to wine,
Nor placed on scales that measure less,
Nor squeezed to fit, nor compromised.
No one can change a single scheduled rendezvous,
Nor by a seamstress's hand be altered or resized.

Each day, a loan he gives
To dress in silk or cast before the swine,
Then asks it back as eve deploys.
That bandits would not steal away the gift he lent,
His borrowed goods destroy.

A rapping comes my windowsill each morn.
I never wake before he wakes.
(He seems to never sleep at all.)
But constantly gives chase day after day
As though I were the only one with whom he had to do.

If magically could be contained his irrepressible pursuit,
I'd ask him come and rest awhile
And watch to my delight a day…a moment stopped.
I'd sit with him in soft converse
And take a breath and close my eyes.

But soon his overwhelming thirst would rise.
That only rushing torrents quench.
And then he'd travel on again,
Collecting everything he sees.
And every tick. His prize.

2009

What if time could be bought and then tucked away for later use? Would that work? If every individual could control the weather, would that work? Of course not. The entire world would be thrown into chaos. And so it would be if we were allowed to control and command time.

# If I Could Stash Some Time Away

If I could buy one pint of time
And hold it in safekeeping
To be retrieved at my command.
I'd carefully plant that precious speck,
Then nourish it
With tenderness,
Anticipating reaping.

A reaping chosen once, just once,
But opened at my asking.
"Choose wisely, son," said Father Time.
"That seed you own will only bloom
The day you wish.
No other day
Can call again my passing."

And so I hold this purchased piece,
A whit for my discernment.
But other moments also pass,
And thousands more remain in line.
Which one to take?
What should I do?
I know, I'll just return it.

2019

Before you were born, time had absolutely no meaning or importance. Time is a treasure hidden away. Life is a thief that allows you to take a tiny portion. But that portion is only a loan of time, and one day it must be given back.

# A Clockwork to Eternity

Amazing how the centuries passed
In years before my day.
Uninterrupted volumes flew,
But I got in their way.

And slowed time down a bit, yet while
The constant trekking drummed,
There was no way to stop or still
That swinging pendulum.

It totters here incessantly;
I've seen the sealed door crack.
Allowing me to come aboard
This train that can't go back.

Each calculation made precise.
All measurements refined.
Securely to my hands attached
This tiny piece of time.

That brings to life a consciousness
That breathes and makes aware
That I've detained a fleeting bit
Of time while I am here.

But when I sleep, this clockwork must
Resume its fast demise.
Till in a blink, that final tick
Will from the eons rise.

2012

# *Life*

Life comes at you in surges, barrages, and heaps
Of true joy or dissembled in grief.
And it makes little difference, a crooked road or straight.
Life's a taker of time and a thief.

Oft it comes on cat paws; hardly noticed we meet
Or at other times thundering herds.
But it just keeps on coming, as swift horseback riders
Stampeding the pass
With lightning for feet.

2016

Ironic, isn't it? Time has a constant speed, and yet it actually seems to go faster and then slower, as if differing limits were somehow attached. Why does this seem so? I suppose no one really knows. It's like some magician's unexplained magic trick. I'm sure you've experienced it in your life.

And time automatically produces aging. Aging is the undesired by-product of time and thus brings about the inevitable demise of youth. Again, how ironic! Once too young to do certain things but now too old.

# The Wizardry of Time

He's always kept the stalking of the kingdom he's been given.
But his presence goes unnoticed for a while.
The clock creeps by. His steps prolong.
No need to rush; alliance to one slower has been made.
A lazy sun falls backward now and then…
Or it would seem. For all is young.
The hours tottering on tortoise feet unhurriedly pass by.
The predator's asleep.
With sword undrawn, he rests for now.

But soon this inching forth explodes to long unbridled strides.
My life, in early days suspended motionless,
Now rises up in hurried flight,
Unaware such suddenness could come.
His grasp, unyielding, presses down.
And too the bindings holding back come loose.
That tranquil dose of early morn
Attaches to an avalanche of tumbling time.
And I, grown older, rush away with him.
Watching days which once crept slow and lazily
Now, unrestrained, whiz by.

2010

# Leaving

When named among the old and aged,
You must indeed be old or near it.
For age can't be disguised too long
Though masks are used to help conceal it.
Can't relegate to storage crates a part for its safekeeping
Nor magically may read again the page already turned.
Can't from the strong man's mighty grip
be snatched away or borrowed,
Nor walk again years' early youth, though every fiber wish it.

So even if you've made yourself somehow someway believe it.
A bird's lost feather fluttering down has no way to retrieve it.
And glacier ice, once broken loose, must drift at sea till melted;
Nor can the loom of cloth once spun spin backward and reweave it.

So journey on amid the swells.
Enjoy each day and cleave it.
For even that, one fleeting day,
You'll turn about and leave it.

2010

# I Used to Be the Wind

I used to be the wind.
When ravens flew, I'd match their beating wings.
Whizzing to a secret place nestled by the sea.
For I could run.

The butterflies waltzed symphonies.
Though I could dance as agilely as they,
Sending breezes to assist their fragile flight,
For I could run... I was the wind.

The arrow from an archer's string.
I, too, once knew that sudden thrust.
Enveloping the open sky
From star to star. For I could run.

Vaulting over field and pasture,
The rush of morning coming
As snowshoes chased by foxes raced,
I'd also run but faster.

And then I'd catch the whirlwind
Until he, panting, rested.
For I could run from sun to sun,
But he, his strength I tested.

I was the cat on mountain peaks
Seen on a ledge, then gone again.
A morning mist soon disappeared
As magically, for I could run.

I felt at times the river's rush
That never slowed or even tired,
Nor stopped aloft cascading falls
But spiraled down in disregard.

I, too, as he, had not observed
How delicate this fleeting gift.
The stream now cuts new canyon walls
That I am unfamiliar with.

I used to be the wind.
But oft betrayed by passing years.
I'm captured by the canyons new design
To gently drift where rushing streams once roared.

And I, as agile as the mountain cat,
Once dancing with the butterfly,
Or challenging the rushing wind,
Once running, now I rest.

Unable to spring forth,
Or course the rivers bend.
Or even run again, although
I used to be the wind.

2004

# Aging's Irony

Because twisters oft ransacked that flat cotton land,
A new cellar was built for protection.
But for most of the time, kids just played on that thing.
Thus, the challenge became my addiction.

Absolutely unclimbable, try as I may.
All the older kids scaled it quite easily.
Some would help me sometimes. But most times, I'd remain
Stuck on ground somewhat lower and measly.

But one summer one evening, one needing one inch,
Quite peculiarly had what I hadn't.
In one leap, I was on it, Mount Everest crowned.
I, a king in his kingdom, now had it.

I climbed up and jumped down with near effortless ease.
Can't imagine ere not being able.
For no obstacles stopped me; no barriers barred
From exploring this climbable table.

My attire, shining armor; my destiny, fame.
Every joust, the uncanny, new victor.
On the high seas, a captain; in blue skies, swift wings.
By whatever confronted, I licked her.

Many years though have passed since that conquering leap.
It still stands there today just as always.
I can't help but take notice how tiny it seems.
But a beast once asleep walks the hallways.

And he taunts as before in an irony deplored
With inanimate brick still contending.
'Cause you know how I couldn't get on as a lad?
Well, guess what…can't get on it again!

2007

Making quilts has always been a fascinating art form to me. You start with very little and then begin slowly collecting pieces and placing them together. With great skill and patience and dedication, a beautiful quilt the artisan created is finally revealed.

My wife quilted. It was easy for her when she first began. But as years passed, her severe handicaps made it increasingly difficult. Each quilt made is different and unique to its maker. And although, as with my wife, every quilter must one day pass, the artistry they leave behind will continue long after its maker leaves.

# Quilters

*Life is like a craftsman who learns to make beautiful quilts.*
*But years slowly take his tools away. So he must*
*then stop work, and soon the quilter dies.*
*But he is fondly remembered by the artistry of his beautiful quilts.*
*(his life)*

We started making quilts some years ago
With children who would never tire.
There were no strangers in that crowd,
For every child became a friend and every friend, a comrade.
Embroidered quilts of finest silk
Was quite an easy thing to do,
But not one child there realized
How precious were those quilts just made
Because the children never stopped to
count the worth of every stitch…
But only played.

Grown older though (no stopping of the
shuttle's clap or wheel from spinning)
The quilts were sewn with greater care
By quilters who but rarely tired.
Yet tire they did and took to rest.
For time assists the children well,
But others, time forgets.
These quilts, made soft of touch and soothing plump,
Were each displayed with love and made
To last through seasons yet to come.
As children, no one cared how fine the thread was weaved or why
Nor felt the garment born anew.
But now each row is skillfully stitched
Until its finally through.

Soon though, alas! The quilters hand began to shake.
First weakening and trembling,
Then tiring every day by noon.
So even stitches bold and colors bright were difficult to recognize.
And more, to realize new quilts could not be made.
For all remains are aged ones,
Formed earlier by younger, nimbler hands.
That unto passing years succumbed,
Where children one time ran.

And now these quilts, so neatly stitched, becoming priceless art,
Are cherished and admired by friends and passersby alike.
The image seen in words and works
Reflects the needle's weave.
So all may know how fine his craft
Before the quilter leaves.

2015

Ever wonder…does time pass at the same perceived speed for everything? Is a day to a butterfly like a year to us? Can birds flock in flight in such perfect symmetry because 30 seconds of time to them is like an hour, with each reacting in unison because their flight seems to be happening in slow motion? Regardless, time nudges along, never hurried nor slowed but perhaps perceived differently.

## Perception

A honeybee buzzed past my head.
I took a swat but missed. Instead,
He flew to lushly clovered grass,
Where seconds quickly fled away,
Then hastened he to honeycombs.
But did to him long hours pass?

On tireless wings the monarch's flight
Proceeded toward enclosing night.
Seems to this navagator years
Surviving on the washing winds
That brought a lifetime filled complete...
How soon to us it disappears.

His house built on the canopy
Took just two sunsets, maybe three.
But if I change, as him become,
The same clockmaker's hand engage,
Transcends a mission pressing years
To build complete this treetop home.

And stars awash on pallets pure
Today remain just as they were
In centuries past. Such time can't send
A morsel to galactic change.
A picture on the canvas stilled
Must be to them the whirlwind.

From start to finish of each breath
That one may take is drawn, then left
To be redeemed, a single jewel
That's harvested from time here spent.
One...diamonds bring; one brings much less.
But each returns his portion full.

And so I ask and contemplate,
Could passing time that God creates
For every creature, everything
(The clock that governs what they do
Though gauged and measured differently)
Perceive its passage each the same?

2011

So time presses ever forward. And all who entertain time must one day meet his offspring—death. Although this nemesis will be feared, to all those faithful to God, his sting will never be felt.

# Pillager

## (1 Corinthians 15:55)

I think about you more these days.
I've come to know you better than before.
My journey takes me closer to your dangerous reef.
But I shall never call you friend.
You've hurt too many of my friends before,
Pouncing on them unaware,
Plundering their goods.
And even now your discontentment propagates toward me.

Although at times I'll sit with you
Politely, not as friends.
Contemplating all the many folks you've entertained,
I'll keep my distance, though, as best I can
Until you draw your welding blade.
Approaching ever near your lair
My portage ore the broad expanse appears.
My fragile steps, hitherto placed safe.
Soon launches forth from tropic seas
Into the icy depths.

But now, oh ancient nemesis you are.
My being shakes no more to go into your dreaded clutch.
For on the battlefront your poison fails.
And so I wait, assured by higher kind.
Forthcoming will my landing gently light
As swan touch down upon an evening's lake.
The long-anticipated venom finds no place.
His music strums the curse he brings.
Though come he must to claim his promised prey.
But where, oh nemesis you are, where lies your awful sting?

2009

But no one can ever know exactly when he will be coming. We cannot know when that final train car will pass by.

# As the Train Passes By

I amble down this country road
To some old railway crossing.
There were no gates nor lights nor bells;
I could have just kept walking.

But speeding on those rusted rails,
A train announced its presence.
I couldn't tell how far it stretched;
A bend hid well its distance.

The porter shouted out, "Stand clear.
More cars may yet be coming."
Their sounds latched on like frosted breath,
And nothing stopped their running.

Some cars a sparkle, polished bright;
Some tattered, parts a missing.
They simply came one after one,
But not one paused while passing.

No clock can gauge the time gone by
Nor order they're arranged in.
Look off awhile or gaze a bit…
No matter…nothing's changing.

Perhaps your train will touch the sky
And span that big…or bigger.
But maybe, just ahead quite soon,
The coachman's lamp will flicker

And leave you on an empty track
Without a day to borrow.
For when that last car leaves, he'll say,
"Your train has passed. Please follow."

2017

## Chapter 2

# God Our Refuge

The time we have here in this world is a gift from our God. There are many other gods: riches, fame, power, etc. But there is only one true living God—Jehovah. And Jehovah our God wants every one of us to live as he has given direction through his Holy Word.

It seems that often it is difficult to understand why certain events happen to us. Why did I lose my job? Why did my car break down? Why didn't I get that promotion? But always remember, if we love God (and by that I mean if we keep his commandments *[John 14:15]*), all things will work together for our good *(Romans 8:28)*. Not all things will be good, but all things will work together and eventually produce good for us.

# Faith

In my kettle when stirred,
Things mysterious rise
That invisibly stroll
Past my wide-open eyes.

Their awakening breath,
No description allows.
For on untraveled paths,
They, in secrecy, browse.

Bringing obstacles forth
That my mind can't explain.
For no compass nor map
Plots the course whence they came.

Inexplicably hung
Twixt an answer and me.
These mysterious things
Only God can decree.

I'll not wrestle with them
Nor give place to their claims,
Casting each in a pot
Till no remnant remains.

Just because I can't see
Doesn't mean that I doubt.
It's just one of those things
That I can't figure out.

2009

## Promotion

There's a quaint, rare profession not many will choose.
For it comes with no fanfare, so most just refuse.
But instead, seek positions of honor and fame.
And if asked to be part of it, promptly excuse.

It will never yield treasures by standards of earth
And, when stacked side by side, seems of minuscule worth.
If suggested, such offers are quickly declined,
Seeking more those promotions of riches and mirth.

They collect golden pyrite, embracing its lure.
But these false misperceptions have wings that can't soar.
Pressed tenaciously on till its value is spent.
Notoriety sought draws one breath…and no more.

This ambition selected means they can't ascend
Up those stairsteps that never turn backward nor end.
For the resume asked for is easily attained
Through devotion to God…then promoted by him.

2014

Not only is God our refuge, the place we go to for safety and protection, he is also our fortress—our stronghold against Satan. God is a faithful friend who will never desert us. Not only will he never leave us, he also gave us a very special gift: a gift to be discussed more and more as we move along.

# If Ever There Were Friends Indeed

*(Exodus 3:14)*

If ever there were friends indeed,
They're friends indeed forever.
Forever love befriends a friend,
A friend, though come whatever.

Search corners far…this sphere…search all.
Search hill and plain but never
Cast from your heart that faithful friend…
"I AM…" your friend forever.

2010
(Original ca. 1965)

## But He Didn't

He could have washed his hands of me.
Salvation…never sent it.
He only had one child to give.
One son…he truly meant it.
And that one son came down to me
From heaven's throne…resplendent.
He could have left me all alone.
But praise his name…he didn't!

2013

Unlike the wages of sin (death), the refuge God offers is absolutely free *(Ephesians 2:8)*. But nothing in Satan's store is free. Everything is extremely expensive. The cost...your soul! Have you ever walked into a store and saw a sign that read: "FREE—TAKE ONE"? Everything in God's gift shop is free. All has already been paid for. And the gift that is given? Eternal life.

# The Gift Shop

The sign on the devil's workshop of sin
Read, "Awaiting your business
Just come right in."
All merchandise glittered with fire from his breath,
Each customer spending
Till nothing was left.

But the sign on God's gift shop right opposite him
(A lighthouse of refuge
No darkness could dim.)
An entrance unlatched. Neither locksmith nor key.
"Just open the door," it read,
"Everything's free."

2010

Such a fantastic gift must be filled with enormous requirements, or so it would seem. But God makes things that seem unreasonable and impossible possible—like dividing the Red Sea or giving sight to the blind with mud or sins washed away through baptism. Contrary to what seems logical and wise, God has designed and fashioned for us all a bridge to salvation that we walk upon by faith.

# Paper Bridge

*(1 Corinthians 1:27–28)*

A paper bridge may not seem fit
To span across this element
Of icy river, frigid lake,
Nor canyons' rising rocks and cliffs.
So many shun its kind rapport
And find another bridge to take.

Those bridges, made of steel and iron,
Bedazzle with deceptive charm.
For rusted bolts are hidden well.
A buttress feigned with flaking paint.
No one believed they'd ever fall.
But so disguised, no one could tell.

The steel, thought strong, was frail and weak.
When simply touched, the beams would creak.
Long cables, s'posed to keep them strong,
Were dangling from the cliffs above.
If even gentle trade winds blew,
A bridge as these would fall headlong.

So trust this paper bridge instead,
Designed to bear the loads ahead.
Inadequate as it appears,
When placed against such mighty steel,
It easily vaults the deep abyss,
And all who cross, those dangers clear.

2015

If we stay faithful to our refuge and unfaithful to the enticing call of the devil, we will be cleansed of our leprosy (our sins) and be made pure, just as Naaman was. *(2 Kings 5:14)*

# Unfaithful to the Serpent's Call

That serpent no excuses made
(I followed him where'er he bade),
For handing me this desolation,
Stretching toward the next creation
Made for himself and kin.

I could have all his charges kept,
For from him warm temptations leapt
That brought with them desired elations
But, for me, became abrasions
No antidote could mend.

So I excused nor bade him well
Nor entered through those gates to hell
But left his feast…to his frustration,
Rescued from his devastation
Whence once my life had been.

2014

# The Maid of Naaman

*(2 kings 5:1–17)*

This little maid,
Her ragged clothes,
The deeds she does,
The God she knows,

Who'd think that such a tiny voice
Could make her captain, plagued, rejoice?
"My Lord can cleanse your rank disease.
Just call on him. He can with ease."

So to the prophet went his camp
To see if God would truly cleanse
And wash away the scourging spots,
Recover new as baby's skin.

No more the groan that lepers wail.
No more the blight of life accursed.
He heeded to the maiden's words,
Then placed her God, Jehovah, first.

This little maid, her confidence
Changed Naaman's life from that day hence.
For he learned well, and so can we
That God alone sets lepers free.

2017

So always trust God as your unfailing, secure refuge. He has cleared the pathway to salvation through his Son, Jesus Christ. He has lit the candle of life, and nothing can snuff it out. Although we often miss the mark, God will deliver us if we trust in him and abide in his sacred Word.

# Candle of Life

Once abided a law
Whence God's hand would recall
Our transgressions, remembering again and again.
But then Christ gave us voice,
So we therefore rejoice
That forgiveness remitted the stinging of sin.

Such a deed thus was done
By God's solitaire Son.
Though defamed, still he came as a shepherd and king
To replace Satan's hate
By exchanging his fate
With the laud of salvation, we joyfully sing.

And our hope, once concealed,
Now by faith is revealed
That no bandit can pillage nor carry away.
Till inseparably moored
With our Savior and Lord
Burns God's candle of life through eternity's day.

2018

# God

For sin, I am repentant,
Although I oft repeat it.
Its beckoning beguiles me,
Its trickery endows me
To do those things I shouldn't,
But praise the Lord, I wouldn't
Dare trust another to
Deliver me but you.

2018

Let me ask, would you consider taking a job that paid a million dollars a day for dusting a single piece of furniture? This unfair, crude analogy can't even begin to compare to the magnificent gifts of God. His Son and our eternal salvation are the ultimate gifts. And if only given the very least of heaven, such a gift will bring eternal joy.

# To Even Be Given the Least Part of Heaven

Oh Lord, I've done but little here;
I haven't earned one thing.
But I will be most grateful, Lord,
If by your grace you welcome me
Into a simple shanty home
That sits beneath your glorious throne.
I'll ask no more. Just give, I pray,
Your very least, oh mighty King…

2020

# Chapter 3

# Caring for Earth

We have been given an important, unique, and irreplaceable responsibility—take care of our planet. All life depends upon the precision God built into earth. When things go wrong, habitat is lost. Water and air become polluted, and extinctions can and do occur. We live on a finely polished jewel of breathable air, drinkable water, and inexhaustible life. And this tiny island of life is the only one known to exist in the vast ocean of infinite space. Earth is our beautiful *garden of Eden*. The Lord God took the man and put him in that garden to till it and to keep it *(Genesis 2:15)*. Should not we also tend and keep the "garden" that has been given to us today? We have the awesome power to either keep it or destroy it. Wiser, more conscientious, caring minds must prevail.

Nature seems invincible. Just look at how she has survived for ages upon countless ages. The circle of earth allows life to exist virtually anywhere on it. There's no upside down or downside up. God's design is perfect. Earth is very efficient when it comes to habitability. It's not a cube or a pyramid, and it's certainly not flat. Earth is a sphere—the perfect shape to distribute gravity. And although seemingly invincible, she can easily be altered or even destroyed either by intent or carelessness.

# Turtle Shell

A tiny ball
About the size of something small
Turns round without a sail or wind
And little to protect at all.
Such meager armament, suppose,
Could not this hapless sphere defend.

Where'er we might
Decide to go, we can despite
Downsides are up and upsides down.
Yet every step comes out just right.
We walk about somehow attached,
By fine design, to solid ground.

Two blazing fires
Besiege our jewel and never tires.
One burns within and one without.
With fierce resolve, their might conspires
To scorch what seems such weak defense…
But staunch protectors stir about.

Their shield…a quilt
Spread out like lace of silkworms' silk.
Repressing flames, the swords repel.
For master builders planned and built
A shelter for this fragile earth
And called it air, our turtle shell.

2019

## Stony Brook

An icy brook found every nook
The woods had not discovered.
It washed stones clean of dirt and things,
Then with some moss re-covered.

It gave a drink to me; I think
I should return the favor.
So carefully I'll come, and be
Upon my best behavior.

Not one step take around its banks,
But first that step be measured.
For brooks are forged from rock and stone
But easily lost…though treasured.

2016

## Pioneer

What paths can still be made
From land and stone already cut?
Who dare to carve their boasting name
As though no man before laid foot?

The twisting Cumberland's been found.
Each river's course explored and named.
These mountains quake 'neath blade and saw.
Wild horses, running free, are tamed.

Great eagles lodge on man-made nests.
Lush plains turned dry by disks and plows.
The pioneer, his mission done,
Has scoured the land...and nature bows.

2015

Like delicate dandelion fuzz, earth floats about. But her outcries cannot be ignored or neglected. Pirates and thieves (that's us) lie in wait, eager to steal and plunder.

# Fragile Island Earth

Without a thought, some careless child
Ignited fire, not knowing how
It feeds unquenched, and then consumes,
Transforming all with hungry plumes
That soon devour and seals his fate
Because the firemen came too late.

2014

# What Pirates Haven't Found

The stream awoke on my approach
(He'd been asleep all night)
To welcome me within my boat.
An absent friend come by.

The ripples tickled him; I'm sure
It brought a laugh and smile.
As I moved slowly down his shore,
He asked me stay a while.

We talked in such a way that some
Could never comprehend.
For visitors were few to come;
Still fewer called him friend.

This stream strolled there deep in the grove
That pirates hadn't found.
Where'er I looked, the bullion strove
To glitter on the ground.

So carefully place your oars and staff
When visiting out here
And tend with care each unmarked path…
This gold could disappear.

2012

We must do what is right concerning earth. Our well-being and existence depend on it. Will forests someday be as rare as the illusive snow leopard? Or will we save our trees? Even a single tree is important. You consider yourself a solitaire being, as someone important. And yet often we don't even care for the children of the world. In nations of plenty, bread is tossed away for ravens to eat. I myself toss it away. Often we don't properly attend to our earth nor to the care of her children.

# Forests

These trees, they listen well.
I come to talk with them.
And they with me, a spell.
I can't explain just how it's done
Nor how I know them, every one.

They stand quite still, like ice filled waterfalls.
Until a gentle wind drops by.
Then breezes see them somehow speak
In noiseless, voiceless languages.

I'm sure they laugh when I respond.
After all, such chattering is something new to them.
Yet we communicate just fine.
Close friends who've been apart too long.

And when the season's right,
Those tattered clothes so proudly worn
Are magically transformed
(Before they don their winter coat)
To garments glittering and bright.

So walk yourself into some untouched forest niche.
I'm sure you'll see
They'll talk to you just like they talk with me.
That is, should you decide to go.
And if the forest sought
(Exploited by their heartless hands
And decimated sorely through the years)
Is even there, as thought.

2020

# The Connoisseur of Doing Right

Three woodsmen walked this mountainside.
There's work that needed done.
An aged tree, whose roots ran deep, for harvesting awaited them.
Its branches held midwinter's snow with ease.
In spring the flowers gathered near. As children roused to play.
Come summer days, its spreading shade subdued a noontide sun.
Ne'er fell a drop of gentle rain unthankfully…not one.

The timber, straight and stretching skyward,
reached for what seemed miles,
Cradling each passerby who chanced to pass that way.
Fruits abounding easily were picked.
Lodging birds and butterflies' lint of the spaciousness she sent.
Never was an evening's guest refused nor found unfit.

But these woodsmen interposed to take that wearied brow.
The weeping hills bowed low, requesting best they could
That the three not take this tree but leave it where it stood
So that no empty sky be evidence of where this fortress rose.

Her roots had gone as deep as they could go.
This aged sage filled up the canopy on high
And spanned crevasses lingering below.
Her fingers held the mountainside that it not wash away
And made the very air those woodsmen breathed.
So please consider hearing as we silently request
That you spare our matriarch and all the land she's dressed.

Then these three woodsmen, certain their intending,
Settled down to rest beneath her shade.
Seeing far beyond the steely axe and chains offending,
These connoisseurs of doing right
Just walked away as evening fell
And left the forest burning bright.

2007

# The Bread We Cast Away

How shall the children learn to be a child
If constant hunger fills their plate?
If nothing more than nothing passes through their quivering lips?
And play's consumed by hidden beasts in wait.

There's bread to spare...but it's elsewhere,
A treasure unabashed concealed
Whose keys have been misplaced
And rust secures the hinge and lock
Till soon the fragrance fades away
And demons lap what little else remains.

The bread lies fresh and baked in baskets full
Across a wide and overflowing table.
But not one slice is given them.
A bridge remains unbuilt.
The ocean's deep; the voyage, long.
The bread lies waste...for no one's able.

And so instead its cast where ravens come to feast.
Their feathers plump and full from what we've given them.
We casually fill these fatted beasts.
But chance not feed the hungry child.
For even of the crumbs do we to them deny
And look the other way...for we ourselves have bread to eat
And thus ignore their every plea
Nor care to feed those starving lives...or even try.

2013

All of God's creation seems to assume that we will always have pure air, clean water, rain forests, lush valleys, and all other wonderful life-sustaining qualities. But only mankind can catastrophically alter those qualities. This globe of ours is absolutely essential to our very existence and indeed the existence of all God's creation.

# Mankind

He breathes in my air…exactly as I.
But each breath he exhales imperils us all.
He leaps in delight as children from school
No longer recalling their teacher by name
Nor what they had learned or been taught them that day.

He lies at his ease, supposing no obligation
To comply to his mission of our dominance.
Taking no thought of the things that might harm us
Nor concern for their dire consequence.

He deems life a triteness
That's ripe to consume.
Is there hope to withstand such a foe?
How soon till his dagger rips open my heart?
Till his sting the last rudiments claim?
These impenetrable walls looming ever before
Bide no means of escape.
For the evening approaches…
And he's still awake.

2008

# The Surrendering of Earth

The crickets sang throughout the night.
"But why?" I asked. "Why bother?"
For dawn was nearing, 'bout to break.
Their chirps persisted, heaven's sake.
And not a single thing got done,
Just cricket songs to one another.

How senseless seemed their piercing sounds.
Someone somehow should smother
The pointless rantings that they make,
For I've grown weary, heaven's sake.
You must have better things to do.
So stop this noise, and I'll recover.

Then dawn stepped in, my saber wield
To wishes, needs, and druthers.
It rips to shreds the moment wake,
These things I've taken, heaven's sake.
And crickets, thought to master me,
Are forthwith crushed, both them and others.

Their songs belie; my reign unleash
The soul of earth, a martyr
That's been destroyed by what I take.
With no regret…nor heaven's sake.
For come this eve their singing stopped.
"You've sealed our fate," they said.
"Why bother?"

2019

# Essential As the Air I Breathe

Beyond the last retreat,
Beyond the farthest stronghold mankind claims,
Or under sudden shade a cloud provides,
Where rushing waters join the mountain's rain
And waterfalls spin diamond threads.
I dare not chance this refuge leave
Nor try to change one soothing sound...
Essential as the air I breathe.

A peaceful morning, dark and still,
Awakes the artist's darting pen,
(He knows exactly where each color goes)
Who watches me watch early light step in.
The brightest stars erased by canopies of blue.
A laden brush my canvas eagerly receives.
Spangling from edge to edge...
Essential as the air I breathe.

So walk this special place with me.
(Unnumbered other worlds supposed)
But here alone, the lighthouse burns,
Embracing voyagers as we.
Unlatch the winds. The hilltops reach,
For few will don these garments weaved.
I find these outposts have become
Essential as the air I breathe.

1984

When the recipe for a delicious plate of food is followed precisely, the dish you'd hoped for tastes wonderful. So it is even as the recipe for the continuation of our current earth is placed before us. We must follow it step by step, ingredient by ingredient if there be any hope of continuing our enjoyment of these very special meals. Else, at some unsuspecting hour, our one and only planet could become unrecognizable. Prayerfully and with diligent care, we can all continue to walk on a recognizable earth, overflowing with life.

## Concerning Earth

We mustn't overcook this soup
Nor change the formula prescribed
Nor chance remove one spice or herb.
This recipe in trust was sent.
We must not alter nor disturb
Aromas filling up our air
But measure each ingredient

And let the kettle's savory broth
Delightfully simmer for a while.
Then cool a bit to please our taste,
For we're attendants to the chef.
A single cup dare not lay waste.
But serve with care each precious dish.
Else evening comes…and nothing's left.

2015

# Isn't This Earth?

Isn't this earth?
Isn't this home?
Am I a voyager taken to live 10 light-years from home?
Where is it I've gone?
When can I return?
I love earth, my home.

This planet I'm on
Owns also a sun.
Though shines not so brightly to light up the day, it must be a sun.
For it wakens each morn
And sleeps through the night...
It must be a sun.

Oceans and seas,
Only a few.
Here on this planet are not even close to any I knew.
Near lifeless and still,
These waters so dark
Could never run blue.

Isn't there snow?
Forests of snow!
Has my trip taken me a distant nebula that hasn't snow?
The wind and the cold
Have taken their share...
But where is the snow?

Often I've seen
Rivers and rills.
They must be lost in this vapor that covers the mountains and hills.
They've all disappeared.
Now desert and dust
Some harbinger fills.

Meadows of grain
Tracing the breeze
Haven't been seen on this planet, they tell me for 200 years.
When can I go home
To earth I adore…
When can I come home?
The answer I fear…

Isn't it strange?
It's not as it seems.
Am I a traveler to constellations or yet to take wing?
The enchantment now gone.
On this land must stay.
I'm walking on earth…
And have been all day.

Circa 1978

# Chapter 4

## Man's Exploration

So we humans have done many things to preserve and many things to harm our little globe. But as it seems to be with humans, we must explore. We must continually attempt to ascend and go a little farther forward. Sometimes, we tend to think of ourselves more highly than we should. At other times we mourn the loss of our failures. But we have always attempted exploration, and suppose we always will.

# This Mighty Ship... Invincible?

The captain, in sumptuous arrogance, laud.
"Nothing can sink her...no, not even God.
She's built to perfection, no flaws, no detection
Of weaknesses on her from aft or to bow.
Her keel's of fine armor, her mask, all withstanding,
Shall weather the greatest storm nature can hand her."
And so they believed, as if they were the maker.
This vessel, invincible, where'er they'd take her.

He lay nearly asleep in that cold, icy water.
*Such folly*, they thought, *why would anything bother?*
But stealthily skulking the ocean's expanse
Till they ever so tenderly brushed with a glance.
Naught at first seemed peculiar...oh, a glass may have tilted.
A chandelier tinkle...but nobody heard it.
Yet doom amassed entry the moment they kissed,
Sending raiders uncounted...no portal was missed.

"Sound the bell! Sound the bell!" Ah, the berg has laid waste.
His dagger, this marksman unerringly placed.
Look how easily felled by this foe unassuming.
None perceived a consuming so effortlessly.
Yet his secret approaching, his presence thus dooming.
The weaponry chosen, a lad with his stone.
Then aroused by the cry of their own desperation.
The vessel lay down to her mooring and home.

The *RMS Titanic*

2007

# Voyager

(NASA probe)

Tiny craft, your fate begins upon the solar wind.
No astronaut has ever been to the places that you've been.
Past Jupiter and Saturn's rings, the strange and unknown loom.
In darkened space, you face the sun,
But only cold consume.

Taken to this distant realm, it's just another star.
No astronaut has ever dared a voyage quite this far.
There's no returning back to earth,
No up or down, no hearing.
Another star creates your day,
Another planet nearing.

Perhaps your flight will take you to enchanted, icy moons,
Past worlds unround, stars yet unfound, past fiery red lagoons.
The mysteries of new galaxies, the seas you ever soar.
We'll never know the lands you touch
Nor where your wings explore.

1981

## Apollo Forgotten

Their ships, a launch to outposts on the moon,
Discovered craft near craters thought unoccupied.
"They've come from some uncharted planet past Andromeda."

"Who was their guide?"
"How long a voyage did they make?"
"What form do you suppose they take?"
"And do they yet with us reside?"
There must be life on worlds afar, beyond Orion's star.

Who can know this riddle of the moon?
How centuries came and passed.
Their memories, buried and forgotten, died.
None living now can recollect or understand
That long ago man left blue earth
And sat *Apollo* in the sand.

1982

# Galactic Gumballs

If God made other life in the fabric of space,
Unfathomable distance would fashion their homes,
Being incomprehensibly far, far away.
Just a flicker and glow from some star's distant ray.

Like big jars of sweet gumballs on very high shelves
Tantalizingly kept in the storekeeper's care.
Yearning children could see them all scattered about,
But despite their attempts, couldn't get any out.

So if life abides elsewhere. God made it, not chance.
(Though the great separator no transport allows.)
Man can only imagine with wonder and awe
How delicious must taste that galactic gumball.

2011

*GTG*

A trailing plume beneath arises,
And all who watch, she hypnotizes.
As thunder wraps those splendid wings,
In one great burst, she moves unseen
Beyond the clouds toward what she prizes.

Such flight demands that laws be tested.
No butterfly was so invested
But simply rides the slightest breeze,
Where condors also glide with ease
'fore reaching distant cliffs still rested.

But for her flight, those rules need bending.
That fiery tongue, her breath ascending
To find among the waiting stars
That every element conspires
To bring about her last descending.

That final gift of flight revealed it.
Those tired and borrowed wings, she yielded.
To never soar the skies again,
Forsaken all those places been.
A brightly blooming flower…wilted.

2015

(The decommissioning of space shuttle, 2011)

# Rider of the Flames

(Space shuttle Challenger)

Igniting of the blazing star
Presses ever unto deeper sky.
Acceleration touches edges of the void
That even eagles thought too high.

Ascending thunderous plumes of sudden flight.
I catch my breath as rockets speak.
And pounding hearts race there beside
To watch your painting of the night.

Shuttle rising, clouds afire.
Unknown the rider waits.
Disguised amid the crew, he breathes.
His summon swells.
His spoils take.

And as we watch,
He vanishes, his bounty pledged to keep.
Their craft on injured wings brought down.
The summit failed,
Taken by the rider's hand
Into the waiting deep.

1986

# Chapter 5

# Losing Loved Ones

Of course, exploration of necessity demands the loss of life. But loss also comes in uncountable other ways. I lost my wife, Donna. For three-quarters of my life, it was always "Gary and Donna." Now it's just "Gary." I've never adjusted to that but continue trying to accept it. And so it is with the loss of others—parents, children, friends, even strangers. One of my first encounters with losing someone was at 18 years old. Jerena was only 5. She became sick and died rather suddenly. She was just a friend. (By the way, I truly dislike the phrase *just a friend*. It makes a friend seem somewhat insignificant.) Jerena was my friend, not "just a friend." I suppose that's one reason I love children so much today. She taught me about the innocence of children and helped me to understand that God cares for all his children, both young and old.

I'll never forget a little girl named Vanessa even though we never met. She was in the ER while my grandaughter was being treated for a small cut. Keira had to get 4 stitches and was fine. But Vanessa didn't make it. She was 2, and Keira, 3. This taught me of just how fragile life can be.

# Vanessa

I met a little child tonight,
Or least it seems I met her
But didn't know her given name,
The color of her hair,
The things she liked,
If pink or white,
Nor of her favorite teddy bear.

Now suddenly she's walking on an unfamiliar road.
The ones she loved no longer walk behind her.
And so I fear she'll be alone.
For no one's able now to hold,
Or searching, even find her.

Oh, that she had a friend or two.
My heart no longer wonder
To know she didn't walk alone
But had at least one other friend
To hold her hand, to comfort, and
At least one wing to gather under.

To know that fear had disappeared,
That just one friend she knew,
And that she wasn't there alone…
To have just one would do.

But she's not with one friend…nor two.
She's counted with unnumbered hosts.
A thousand angels gather round.
To show ten thousand wonders found,
Each treating her as royalty,
Attending to her every need.

And oh, lest I by chance forget
(Ten thousand angels won't quite do),
For Jesus, holding tight her hand,
Is right there with her too.

2014

Donna, my wife, contracted a vicious disease when she was only 22. Over the years, it slowly and painfully invaded her. But Donna was a flower of a different kind. Most flowers grow and bloom in lush well-watered soil. Hers struggled and grew in arid sands, yet the flowers that bloomed were lovelier than any other. And despite her constant struggles, she continually sang. I can still hear her today, singing praises to God for all her blessings. Through all her conflicts, her contentment and faith was amazing. She continues to joyfully sing but accompanied by angels in heaven now.

# Flowers of a Different Kind

Without a threat nor perils touched,
The bayou flaunts its dazzling plumes,
While others bow 'neath desert's heat
That oft assault their fragile blooms.

No crowns to dress or decorate
Nor pedestals to rest upon.
The midday's sun's relentless siege
Belies the ardent path they've gone.

These parched and thirsting flowers stand
Against an ever-present foe.
Yet lovelier their petals spread
Than those within the bayou grow.

2017

# With Wings...and Other Things

Her transport there consists of wings,
Though they require no beating.
For heaven's air just lifts her high,
While other joys creating.

Seems time has lost its residence,
And good resides exhaustless.
She easily flies from place to place,
Delightful wonders crosses.

No heart can fathom such a home,
Its shores an endless river.
Seems God made everything just right,
And now its glory gives her.

2016

# Her Angels Sing in Heaven

I listened to her every song,
An orchestra and chorus
That soothed away her cares and fears
Like raindrops soothe the forests.

Those simple verses' melodies
Prevailed from morn till evening,
Exactly what her heart had sought,
A new spun yarn for weaving.

But soon, so soon, the weavers loom,
In disrepair, laid silent.
No more the hand-wound yarn and thread
Could weave, nor could one find it

As if her jewels were swept away,
As if the raindrops taken.
Now even forests weep aloud,
Their fragile world shaken.

A stillness seals those songs she sang.
No portal can retrieve them.
For they, and she, have gone away.
In silentness, she leaves them.

Just look how much those lovely psalms
Brought rescue from her anguish.
But now, no more, the music's gone.
In silent halls, they languish.

So angels said, "We'll sing with you
A chorus God has given."
And underneath the tree of life,
They sing her songs in heaven.

2018

My dad, Hallie A. Scott Jr., served on the battlefront in World War II. And as you might suspect, he never talked much about it really hardly ever. But he did relate a few stories.

He and some other soldiers were in a barn. Dad was leading the way out when he stopped to tie one of his boots. Another soldier then took the lead. As that soldier cleared the barn, a German sniper shot him dead. My dad and the others then made a quick escape. Without that untied boot, I wouldn't be here today.

On a cold, snowy winter day, his platoon was ordered to take a ridge. They desperately tried, but snow became so deep on their side of the hill they couldn't advance. Another platoon on the other side was then ordered to go, but the Germans were waiting for them, and that platoon was wiped out. Without that deep snow, I wouldn't be here today.

And once they were pinned in a beet field. A petrified, horrified soldier was ordered to hand carry a message. Dad saw his fear. He volunteered to deliver the note. He would zig and zag, take shelter in the beets, then zig and zag some more. He eventually made it through. Without those beets, I wouldn't be here today.

Dad cared for his family with the same dedication he had as an American soldier.

## The Forgotten Decoration

Liberator, your daring deeds unspoken still,
  Allowing me unfearful life.
Honors due but never given, now we cite,
  For none can seize the cup we drink.
No sentry trace our morning walk,
  Nor soldiers seal the night.

He fought for treasures that the predator desired.
  (A fragrance riding mountain winds
Cannot be held by others' will nor by decrees withstood.)
  So now I walk unguarded trails
Or splash my feet in cooling streams.
  (Though no one said I could.)

To him whose hands forged liberty,
  A gleaner of these precious things,
Who stood against that dreaded beast untamed,
  In debt to you for such a prize,
Which surely now do consecrate,
  And freedom is its name.

(For my dad, who served on the battlefront during World War
II but received absolutely nothing for it. Oh, on the day of
his discharge, he did get seven dollars for a bus ride home.)

1985

My mother loved children. The kids she would babysit all called her Aunt Myra. She loved her three sons, and she loved her grandchildren and great-grandchildren. However, there was one great-granddaughter she was never allowed to meet or love. They were butterflies born in different seasons because her train (riding trains was another thing she loved) had already left.

# Two Butterflies

(Keira and Granmummy)

A butterfly came fluttering to entertain the crowd.
Each pirouette was magnified with eyes of adoration
On newborn wings that took her first to one and then another.
Each promenade and curtsy made would resonate applause.

Shan't she ask for anything, for everything was given.
Her captivating smile became a sweetened wine to them.
And all who gathered sipped this drink of joy and jubilation
That pleased their taste, each cupful laced with her intoxicants.

But years ago, another danced as does this ballerina.
And even so, the two of them had only danced alone
Since long before this yearling dancer first awoke to dancing.
On aging wings already she had folded hers in rest.

An ocean blue without sunrise or sunset to enrich it.
A mountain left uncovered by embellishments of snow.
All by themselves, their beauty was quite obvious to any.
But blended in the kettle, fragrance would the whole room know.

Two butterflies…one flying now, one flew in years a-passing.
That precious seed and germ of love in different pasture grown,
The arc of time has drawn a line that keeps them separated.
But think what music be composed had they each other known.

2011

# The Train to Albuquerque

Her bags lay at the railway stop,
Each neatly packed as usual…
No one thought she would be leaving.
No one thought departures made
By the stationmaster's summon
At this unexpected call.

Her soft blue coat blew in the breeze
Beside that rustic depot bench.
Her eyes gleamed in anticipation,
Clutching close her reservation,
Listening for the whistles sounding
Of the journey to begin.

A soothing stillness filled this morning,
Warming aught that foggy day.
"All aboard," the linesman cried.
(His opened pocket watch beside him.)
"All aboard…this train's departing…
Albuquerque's far away."

And as the engine left the station
(Its smoke and steam had scarcely cleared)
One final hill, then in a moment,
That little train just disappeared.

(To my mother, she always wanted to take a long train ride.
Now she's on her way.)

2005

She is now a beautiful lilac, but her flower will never wilt.

# The Lilac Flowering

"We have a pretty place," she'd say.
"The trees all seem content right here beside us,
Waiting for a chance to scatter shade about.
It's such a lovely place.
Just count the joys, the beauty 'round us
And cherish moments near or years so quickly passed."

"We have a pretty place," she'd say.
(Though only borrowed for a moment
from another's vault of goods.)
A carmine sunset melting in an evening sky so briefly kept.
Softly calls the whisperer,
Vanishing in silent steps within the night's domain.

For yesterday, a young man came twixt midnight's bell and morning
And bade her walk with him.
"I have a pretty place," he said,
"Of flowers' constant blooming."
Imagination hasn't chanced upon such lovely shores.
Its fragrance drifting everywhere as ships at dock or sailing,
Whose latitude and longitude no compass finds
Nor maps and charts its secret way reveals.

Allaying waters soothed her faltered steps,
For they were failing.
And everything descried or heard or touched
Were chords choirmasters never plucked
But, now in pure magnificence, are strumming.

"I have a pretty place," he said,
"Where timelessness awakens.
Where farewells never rouse
Nor sadness enters at your gate or hacienda door.
Come see these streams of quiescence and blue.
My weary traveler, come see my lilac flowering.
Come see, my faithful voyager.
I've made this all for you."

2005

Both of my parents had very hard times in their childhoods and early marriage. Even as we three boys were in school, she picked cotton to buy us clothes. Dad delayed his senior year of high school to help his dad clear land with axes and handsaws. The pay was one dollar a day. But despite the hard times, they always managed to help others. Now these two beautiful diamonds have been lost in the sea, but their value to me will always be held dearly.

# The Settlement of Lauratown

Dad pronounced it <u>Lourietown</u>: his birthplace in Arkansas [1921] that
no longer exists. He first told me about Lauratown a few years ago. It
was located just south of Portia and just north of Clover Bend along
the Black River. Clover Bend also seems to have vanished. The name
is so unassuming, reminding me of his calm, caring, unexcitable ways.
Lauratown and his own easygoing nature now mingle together.

I wasn't there to see that little village built
Each dwelling formed of hand-split rails.
Each seed laid deep in harvest's hope.
A furrowed road the laden wagons rend.
And care a backyard gardener showed,
Whose flowers never failed.
A helping hand they'd offer oft
To foreigner and friend.

The townsfolk talked of all the good God did for them
(While wiping sweat from limb and brow).
For all the sunny days their thirsty crops drank in.
The love they shared…
For knees that bowed…
For home to evening's rest.

They met to raise a neighbor's barn the twisters took from him.
From rise till set, the work ensued.
To only help in time of need was all the payment made.
Their heartfelt deed, as silent rain,
The sounding trumps forbade.

That village, planted long ago, seemed
rooted strong as elm and oak,
So no one thought to photograph
Those tattered gates and whitewashed fences weaving round
Nor stash a picture of the old mills grinding stone
The embers fluttering and faint
Until that final spark remaining flickered and went out.

Now nothing's left to keep this town awake.
The riverbed dried up some years ago.
Those creaking floors, announcing someone's coming,
Lie ever hushed of footfalls' constant drumming.
Once bustling streets are clad in planted crops.
And marketplaces ride the passing wind.
Nothing's here of crowds once teeming
'Round the church's steeple's singing throng.

Smoke from chimneys used to drift through winter's chill
Now settles elsewhere undetected.
Reluctant memories find it difficult to venture out.
All the chamber music has been sung.
Her lantern oils finally burnt.
No children's joy…no tears remain to weep.
And none, save God, can now recall
Those selfless deeds that love outpoured.
For Lauratown has nodded off to sleep.

2005

# Two Diamonds

I once held diamonds in my hand.
One was large; the other small.
But you know, size really didn't matter, not at all…
For they were treasure maps and guiding stars to lead me home
And taught me understanding right from wrong.

A lot can change to a lot of things.
But my two diamonds never changed.
Their polished edges fit as smooth inseparable stones
That I'd roll within my hand to feel that crystal cut
Precisely sculpted by their builder's hand.

I loved the sounds they made…
Water splashing, snowflakes falling,
A summer's rain parading on my roof all night.
Watching them was watching flocking birds
Moving synchronized and effortless in seeming single flight.

But one day, not long ago, the little stone
(The one I'd always watched with special care)
Slipped between my fingers' clutch.
Beyond retrieving, none could touch with even outstretched arms.
My musical sonata fell to silence as I watched it tumbling away.
And no persuasion, no debating
Could bring it back again or have it stay.

An orchestra's rendition played to missing violins.
Clouds that bring no rain.
A harbor's ships each gone to sea, leaving no one to defend.
Who once held two, holds only one.
A misplaced article that's never found
Though every crack and crevice be explored.

Diamond. Diamond in my hand.
I weep for all the loneliness you've taken in
And loneliness in eggshell vessels yet to burst.
Your sails, once filled with overflowing winds,
Now lap in gentle breeze that barely carry you along…
A solitary beacon shining through surrounding night.
Alone here in my hand…
The little one is gone…

You also must depart, it seems.
(Even tall ships disappear beyond horizons thought so far away)
Surging depths beat constantly against your bow.
The current draws you ever seaward.
Your mooring to the bay is lost somehow.

I'm standing all alone upon this beach.
Diamond clutching in my hand, you've also slipped away,
Finding passage through the shoals
Till once again these diamonds meet.

2005

And so this cycle will continue. Individuals, families, tribes, civilizations will come and go, become unrecoverable, and then sadly, probably forgotten.

# Empty Canoe

(A simple life from days gone by, now forever vanished)

His birch canoe can't find its way
To ancient flowing rivers
But harbors silently alone
On unfamiliar land.
His mighty bow has no one left
To draw its blazing arrows,
Like tethered hawks that once soared high
Or foxes snared that ran.

Wouldst I could go and find again
The owner of this vessel?
Those forested hills and endless plains
Have, as the wolf, lain down.
His buffalo, once millions strong,
No longer roam the prairie.
So, too, the keeper of this craft
Though sought, cannot be found.

2015

# Chapter 6

# Life's Journey

As you know, life will always have its ups and downs. The trick is to overcome the downs. This is done with persistence, with inner strength, and of course with God. Like any journey undertaken (a walk in the woods or a voyage around the world), prepare for it, enjoy it, and give it your best effort. Obstacles will undoubtedly arise, but each can be defeated with the right tools.

All roads lead to one final destination—eternity! Life here on earth is just a loan: something we borrow for a short time. God will ask for it back one day, so be certain to properly attend to it with care and love.

## The Township

The town sits quietly close to here,
Though you may not have sensed it.
No matter what the road you're on,
This township's not too distant.

No detours or delays confound;
All signs point one direction.
So everyone on every road
Comes to this same location.

The lantern flickers off and on;
It's hard to judge the distance.
You could arrive at any time...
Perhaps today, for instance.

Enjoy the ride; you've been obliged
To make your reservation.
For once, life's journey has begun
This town's your destination.

2012

# *It*

It dangles on silk that could break any moment,
Erupting as sparks from a flame without notice.
Though placed in your hands for a while, you don't own it.
The contents are borrowed; you've simply been loaned it.

Sometimes it flies by like balloons in a circus.
The clowns in their costumes perform without purpose.
At other times, kings build grand castles in minutes,
Then leaving, not seeing the beauty there in it.

One day, it floats effortlessly without bending.
Another, with battles, it's always contending.
It never sleeps soundly…in fact, takes no sleeping,
For lookouts to dangers must always be keeping.

It circles desiring, unsure where should land it.
But suddenly plunging, comes in as a bandit
Who gathers up goods to its liking and passion
And dresses to please in its own chosen fashion.

Although it's been leased or on loan or just rented,
Entrusted to you…you're the one who was lent it.
Each contract expired will require yet another
To reach toward forever, perhaps even further.

So temper with goodness; bring all to subjection.
That evil be stifled; make God your selection.
To journey with him through this life and the next one.
That no interference obscures your conviction.

This thing we call life, we all have one…but just one.
Parading about in a custom-made costume.
Don't mind that ten billion or more have been issued.
Just care for the only one out there that is you.

2014

## Cabin Home

My cabin nestles in the woods.
Has been for quite some years.
You'll never find it hard to find.
A chimney beckons come inside.
The brush has all been cleared.

I walk along its threadbare path.
Each step grows steeper still
To draw of water needed there.
For promised rain delayed its call,
And I have cups to fill.

Young winter, rousing raiding storms,
Has brought the icy wind
That penetrates these shanty walls.
Permitting entry here and there
Through cracks I can't attend.

When come the rains, the rain comes in
'Bout shingles patched before.
And chill that oft disturbs my sleep,
Naps by the fire, it's presence creeps
As visiting the more.

There's much to do ere putting out
This midnight lamp I burn.
Each article I must arrange.
The soiled floors, the mantle clean
And borrowed things return.

This cabin home I'll tend with care,
Though gathers night about.
And when the landlord asks it back,
I'll close each door, secure each hasp,
And snuff my lantern out.

2008

Satan is a roaring lion, seeking to devour anyone and everyone. It is imperative to eliminate him as your ball of yarn unwinds. So cast the devil away, and he, being the coward that he is, will instantly flee.

# Scat

(James 4:7)

When Satan comes calling, comes looking for me,
With poisonous venom,
With lies to deceive,
With cups full of evil,
Containers of hate,
He comes noon or midnight
To plague me...
But wait...

When I see him approaching, though shrewdly disguised,
Tiny wisps of his bravery from embers arise.
For I bid him be gone,
And his courage betrays.
When confronted, he runs
Without pause or delays.

But beware though, he's like icy water that creeps
Through the smallest of cracks
Till the occupants reach.
So I nail the loose shingles.
Repair the torn eves,
Taking refuge against his despicable deeds.

Then he stops uninvited and hastily flees
From my watertight home,
For a toxin I've found
That has left him of late quite allergic to me.

2018

# Shattered Bottles

*(1 Peter 5:8)*

My bottle's filled with ugliness
Securely kept in dark stained glass.
It won't pour through the open spout.
Though tilted down, it won't come out.

When sipped or drank, it fills back up.
Some genie must live deep inside
Who loves the bottle's bitter taste
And keeps it full, not one drop wastes.

Its content rises to the brim
With awful taste and awful things.
He truly loves this residence
And clings with ridged fingers, hence,

The only way to rid myself
Of all this ugliness inside
Is cast it down on rocks and stones,
Where shards become the bottles bones.

And what it held comes gushing out.
The genie simply runs away
To find another dark stained glass.
Another one…but not his last.

2015

# My Alcoholic Friend

I have this friend…he drinks a lot.
Oh, not of wine or chardonnay
Nor whiskey from the bottle briskly poured.
He drinks instead of other awful things
And can't control the anger vent from them,
Nor does he try.

Disregarding friends and kin,
Indulgences consume each move he makes.
Paying dues to those whose tantalizing cups
Are alien to anything that's good.
He relishes these moments spent
As though they were a castle built for him.
A castle built of tender, readied for the kindling of fire.

If you could help my poor, decrepit friend
That soon this plague be banished whole.
I'd kindly thank the effort you extend
To heal such dreadfulness
And overturn his crippling intoxicants.

But you mustn't linger long.
Instead, move quickly, else his seizures come
And of your goods take anything they please.

No other can contain if such a one must drink.
No aid administered by others can redeem.
Himself alone must find the hidden antidote
And take thereof the cure prescribed.
None other can.

And now from this acquaintance close,
I yearn to unacquainted be.
For this, my alcoholic friend...
Whose cravings unrelentingly enslave...
Who walks beside each step I take...
My alcoholic friend...is me!

2010

Bullies will likely enter life. One of my first bullies was Mayo. He really had it in for me, but to this day, I don't know why. Phillip was another. I withstood Phillip with the help of what Mayo had taught me. Eventually, Phillip and I played together on the basketball team and became friends. There have since been many Mayos and many Phillips, but with courage and with the help of God, they can all be defeated.

# Mayo Rider

(The kid who made me brave)

He had a most uncommon name,
Though never told him that
'Cause that might get my face smashed in,
Which I could do without.

Mayo didn't like me much.
Just why, I didn't know.
I wasn't nearly tough as he.
(His ego, I suppose.)

The campus there at LHS
Sprawled out a city block,
Which gave me lots of room to run
And shiver in my boots.

I'd hide 'mong friends and make excuse.
Escape routines rehearse
Because he said he'd beat me up
If given half a chance.

So I steered clear of Mayo's threats,
Which seemed sure doom for me.
While counting down long minutes till
The recess bell would ring.

Then one day it occurred that he
Could have a hundred times
Demolished me from limb to limb!
He never did...but why?

Perhaps his talk was only talk,
A mere display and threat.
Perhaps he kinda feared me too.
Perhaps...but just not yet.

Regardless, I've braved up since then
And taken in account
That other Mayos live out there,
Though not a clue where at.

But when they choose to visit me,
I'll never fear a one.
'Cause Mayo Kider made me brave
When others like him come.

2011

Life proceeds. It's like a ripple on water or climbing a ladder—life goes on. But the farther one goes, the smaller becomes the ripple and the more difficult it becomes to climb up an ever-weakening ladder.

# A Ripple on the Pond

A ripple on the pond
Awakened by a stone tossed in.
But even so, the instant born
And by the very water formed
Returns to whence it first sprang up
Without a trace where it had been.

It seemed when first beget
To form an ocean's crested wave,
To strike out boldly and consume
Each corner of this small lagoon.
Till coming near the distant shore,
The pond took back the gift it gave.

And so, as they, are we
A stone cast in to briefly view,
A tiny splash that comes, then fades,
Replaced by newer ripples made
From other stones at other times
That came as we…then vanish too.

2017

# Stepping Up the Ladder's Rungs

One ladder rung when life was young.
When life first visited, brand new.
But slowly years passed quickly by,
My daughter came. I then claimed two.

That's not so high on ladder bars.
But life bewilders constantly.
My children's children shared her place.
So I climbed on, unscathed, to three.

These steps, meticulously scaled,
Rise upward from this earthen floor.
More generations followed me.
And just like that, I stood on four.

Rung five looms difficult to reach.
And six, no wealth attained can buy.
A ladder such becomes quite weak
When stretched to elevate that high.

So standing on this current step
Could be the last my journey takes.
For who can tell how many more
I shall ascend before it breaks.

2019

Each and every one of us has a living soul, and that soul will live forever. So that makes me pretty special—just like you. We are all seeking heaven when things get finished here—a life that is somewhat incomprehensible. After all, we accept it only by faith.

## Forever

Some things will last though ages pass.
I know a few.
I've added up the number here
To know what volumes be.

But counting them, to my surprise,
It's more than I supposed,
So I'll just write them down, each one,
So you can easily see.

First of all, of course, there's God.
His Son, the Word, sits right next him.
The Spirit intercedes for us throughout life's tangled forests,
And, too, the heavenly angel bands sing in eternal chorus.

Guess that's 'bout all; my list is done,
Far shorter than supposed.
For what had seemed an open door
Quite suddenly was closed.

For life unending stands select
Outside the constitute of death
That only God can orchestrate,
That only he can contemplate.
Such special love, such special care from high must be endowed
Before a solitary thing eternity's allowed.

So I conclude my tiny list
Of those that time will not be rending.

But wait, there's more, lest I forget
Our living souls will see no ending.

2018

# *You*

You're special too…like me; so are you.
For you're the only you who's ever been.
And you alone compose a masterpiece
That even kings and queens and princes cannot write.
For they are they; and you are you,
An incandescent, shining soul-illuminating night.

Ten million stars appear the same
When viewed through distant eyes.
But each of them possess a name
And holds a special place reserved within the populated skies.

When snowstorms rage, no single flake
Can turn the bower white.
And yet it takes each one to make
The village look exactly right.

So too are you, designed and rare,
Embroidered with a seamstress's skills
That no one else these garments wear.
For you alone their priceless worth reveals.

2016

# Blue Marlin

A tiny fish caught on my line.
I know each weave and bob he makes
And how he rests from time to time
Or from the seabed floor awakes.

But should a marlin shake my pole
With unacquainted dives and leaps,
I'd have no clue which way he'd go
Nor of the hours that he keeps.

My present life's that fish I caught.
The marlin, life that's yet to be.
No hook can catch such fishes sought.
For marlin swim another sea.

These little fish we know quite well.
The ocean's stocked with lots of them.
And yet, despite the seas we sail,
No fishers fish where marlin swim.

2016

We are all now working on our eternal "retirement." The road will often be bumpy and rough, while at other times smooth and gentle. Be diligent, be dutiful because this "retirement plan" has no equal.

# *Hiring*

Acquiring work, I loved my job.
It satisfied my wants and wishes.
Of course, some days were drab and plain,
And some had even worse conditions.

I forged my way through good and bad,
Until that day of my retiring,
Then found to great delight and joy
Another place already hiring.

My résumé was sent ahead,
Contained therein a lifetime striven.
And sure enough, they hired me.
A perfect job…and it's called heaven.

2015

# The Great Circus Ball

I took my turn riding the great circus ball
Made of thread and torn fabric, of poison and gall.
My fond wishings stood helpless to turn it aside,
For the course that it chose was the course I must ride.

I stayed on just the same, on that shadowy globe
And went where'er it wandered…atop it I rode.
Unpredictable turns took me places unmapped,
Driving deeper and deeper to perils like that.

Just as suddenly though, inexplicable change.
Please forgive if I sound quite elated.
For I stand on another, another great ball
Now transformed into something most lovely created.
Continuing on in a smooth, silky ride,
All the briars and sharp brambles pass by to one side.
Here, the wind's at my back.
Here, the songbird's awake.
In such days of contentment, I stand most content
And consume all the honey this honeycomb lent.

'Tis a fine circus ball, this great one I'm on.
But I know just as rapidly it could be gone.
Back to rust and decay, back to shadows and gloom.
For awaiting are heartbreaks just in the next room.
So I'll cling to the morsels and tittles therewith.
Cherish every day, riding this circus ball gift.

2006

# Chapter 7

# Lies and Deception

Oh yes, deception, cruelty to others, and lies are very much a part of the journey through life. When people choose to replace good with evil, the results are always undesirable. It all began when Satan deceived and lied in the garden, and it will not end until Jesus returns.

Lies have no boundaries. They spread like a virus, infesting truth. Lies can't change truth but, through deception, can make it appear differently. Once it does this, lies can and will produce multiplied offspring.

# Lies

Lies are pieces of truth that's been turned inside out
Or bright colors washed dull till they blend.
Lies can make truth look small when comparing indeed
Become merely a drop…not the sea.

For when truth is diluted with trespassing lies,
Even trust in what's trusted gives way.
Keeping diligent watch of each false confidant,
Their persuasive deceptions invade.

So beware their sweet taste, how they painlessly sting.
For a lie can be most anything.
With unerring resolve, its dishonorable task
Is to take truth and stash it away.

2018

# Thunder

When thunder comes, the deed's been done,
The spark already laid.
For thunder's only relevant
Of some far sinister event
That looming storms had made.

A pillager of fleet resolve.
A nimble northern wind.
Had not that lightning ever come,
In silence would this drummer drum,
Nor morning's peace offend.

But once ignited by his flame,
The restless offspring rise
To cut to shreds the docile dawn.
Tell everything it rests upon
That thunderous host decries.

No force can cage, nor strength suppress.
No wish nor want repel.
Untethered by its timely birth
To cover the expanse of earth
Wherein it chose to dwell.

And such are lies as lightning's flash
Infests unwary heirs
So each, when freed, breeds consequence,
Like thunder born of lightning, hence.
A lie unleashed ensnares.

2018

# Hyenas

My son's a leopard.
I am too.

Both stealth and strength accompany him.
He takes his fill throughout the night.
I think it well; I think it right.
For he's my son, and all he does, I justify.

But come hyenas for their share.
The very part my son so takes.
I cringe to see them stalking near.
They're not my kin; they oft offend.
Despise I every one of them.

"Why can't we come?" some dare to ask.
What leopards take, hyenas take.
But leopards bear no consequence.
The lamb and calf for mercy cry,
Yet leopards come without refute
And fill their empty bellies full.
While from the same savannah grass,
Hyenas hunt as leopards do.
But not one coming here may pass.

They're not as leopards, not at all.
They're not our sons nor of our race.
To kin no fault is ever seen.
For kin's like us, and us like them.
Not like that pack we so deplore.
So why accept or show respect
To any cursed hyena sect?
With every breath, with all our strength,
Despise we them the more and more.

But why? Again they asked, but why?
You justify what leopards do.
Perhaps it's different fur they dote.
But what is done need not be judged by likes or wants
Nor by some strip or spot approve.
Hyenas hunt what leopards do.
They simply wear a different coat.

2015

## "I Just Want Christmas"

(Spoken by one of the Sandy Hook children)

Cowardice awoke today,
Mingling with innocence,
Contaminating soft blue skies
With bellowings of senselessness
That indiscriminately choked these little ones
And those around.

He took from them as from a babe.
He took the best they had.
Their budding lives…he stole each one
But couldn't steal their hearts and souls.
God took each one with him
And wiped tears dry.
Their fears erased,
It's Christmas every day.
No strangers knock. No doors need locked,
For only love and kindness comes their way.

But as for cowardice, no place for him allowed.
No place to run…no place to hide from judgment's mighty hand
A coward of the cowardly.
With misery on misery, he miserably crawls
On roads of hopelessness and shame.
From life unfit, he further falls.

Unconscionable, his fate spewed out.
By those disgraced, them he disgrace and shun.
Satan's angels sore despise and buffet him.
Even now, before a living God must stand…
Face-to-face,
Eternity to reckon with…
And there's no place to run.

2014

Have no place for Satan, the prince of this world. Desert him and leave him all by himself on his isle of lies. Not only is he a liar, he is the father of liars *(John 8:44)*.

# Intruder at My Door

Outside my door, the wizard whispered,
"Please let me in… I won't stay long.
I only wish to warm my hands
And maybe taste your brewing soup.
I've other places yet to go.
I'll stay awhile, then I'll be gone."

His tantalized persuasiveness entreated me
To let him in (but just this once).
He'll taste my soup and warm his hands.
That's all he'll do…he told me so,
Then quickly go and leave me be,
His deviltry gone far away to someone else's home.

Many years have since been snatched away,
And I recall those promises he made
To warm his hands and taste my soup
And rest awhile upon my porch
Then find another's unlatched door
To take his refuge in.

But rising every morn, I find him still around,
Slumbering upon my couch,
Pillaging my goods,
Drinking from my garden spring,
Intruding even where bold thieves and robbers fail.
He's still around. He hasn't left…
And I suppose he never will.

Yet I alone invited him to come, and so he did.
Consuming every ounce he could
Till nothing else remained.
And now he laid his claims to every room.
On all I own he stamps his seal.
On perches high he watches me…
And I suppose he always will.

2009

# A Prince Refused

*(John 12:31)*

There lives a prince I used to know.
His kingdom's like no other, though.
He beckons subjects freely share
His lavish wealth of wickedness.
It gleams like gold and ruby stones
Within that deviltry he owns.
Disguised, realized too late a foe
As he, on common pathways, go.
This scourge of scourges never rests.
His curse come up from hades's depths.

No man is free from such a prince.
Demands he more than recompense.
When tallied up, the debts and dues
Are multiplied by score times score.
Not only does he lie, he cheats.
His evil ways tenfold repeats.

So seek instead a mighty king
Who'll vanquish every debt you bring.
A prince refused, his deeds deplored,
For Christ, our King, that prince destroyed.

2019

# Chapter 8

## Freedom and Truth

Freedom is truth, and truth is freedom. (And ye shall know the truth and the truth shall set you free *[John 8:32]*.) Neither should be trifled with nor taken for granted. A high price had to be paid for both our physical and spiritual freedom, and both should be handled with care and thanksgiving.

Remember Secretariat, the thoroughbred racehorse? He could swiftly run the dirt at Church Hill or graze lush bluegrass pastures in Kentucky. We think of that as freedom. Yet Secretariat had to be given loving, tender care. Just one misguided step could have been disastrous. Freedom can also just as easily be snuffed out.

# Tremendous Machine

There's been many a colt since this chestnut first ran.
Many more will undoubtedly come.
Speeding hoofs that they sought
Were much faster than thought.
So he easily outdistanced each one.

As the thoroughbred challengers called for his name,
They just flailed in his thunder and dust.
Breathing air not yet breathed,
No one really believed
He could run with the wind, but he must.

When the circle was closed, Secretariat rose,
None before him nor since have we seen.
His magnificent stride,
Dirt and turf thrown aside,
He moved like a tremendous machine.

2015

# Even Gentle Wind

Freedom is a candle burning
Though scarcely kept alight.
That fragile flame it rests upon
Can only shine so bright.

If even gentle winds disturb,
It flickers all about.
Imagine though should storms arise.
That candle could go out.

Like connoisseurs of gourmet feasts,
Whose careful measurements
Reveal the fragrant sprinkling
Of fine ingredients.

Our freedom we must also tend.
No crumb nor fragment waste.
For if forsaken, freedom too
Will lose its pleasant taste.

2019

The freedom that we now enjoy was fought for long and hard. The prize won is one of the most valuable that can be had. We walk when and where it pleases us. Nothing separates or divides. With a continued desire and effort, truth and freedom will prayerfully keep dining with us, and us with them.

## *Forefathers*

I haven't much to do round here,
Just tend this carved out trail.
The fox and squirrel sure don't mind
The easy way it goes.

When morning sun meanders through
The loosening prongs of night,
I take the time to watch him spin
This little trick he knows.

The tireless beaver's magic lake
Makes play of river wilds.
Perhaps I'll linger near his bridge
Or on his lodging nest.

For jagged cliffs and bramble plain
Have all been neatly shorn.
Allowing me to leisurely
Ascend or simply rest.

So dutifully the turning earth
Splits day from night's wind wail.
And there is not much else to do.
Save breath this fragrant air

Which brings the laden ships to port
To anchor calm and safe
Can aught but thank the shoresmen for
Each lantern burning there.

Yes, many folded flowers bloom.
Their polished diamonds gleam.
So grab your hat and coat and come.
Don't search; the treasure's here.

From unknown friends, now safely stored.
Meticulously kept.
Through storms and battles fought and won,
We hold it always near.

2008

# A Walk in Backwood Woods and Free

These lines I write in secrecy,
Afraid who might consume their thought.
Unsure the plight I might disturb
Should one unknown contract a word,
Reminding I'm no longer free
To even walk these lovely woods
Or sail upon my native sea.

Each thought, kept silent, stills my pen.
This dreadful beast my words suppressed.
For no one knew it could escape
To take this thing called liberty.
And no one thought that tiny seed
(Sprung up unrecognized within)
Would soon infest from shore to shore
By raising up this dreaded breed.

Where stallions ran, now fences rise.
Contained, the rushing river dies.
I must win back this given right
And evil cast into the night.
The words unsaid must now be said.
The verse unwritten now be read.
I pray a morning soon may be
(That if I wish, if I so choose)
To sail again my native sea
And walk these backwood woods,
And free.

1984

# Walls

They built a wall to keep others out,
But now they've locked me in.
And freedom fought through blood and tears.
Reluctantly lost, I rescind.

"Come share our gift of sweet liberty.
We welcome all," they said.
But shadows from this towering wall
Cast darkness upon me instead.

Like ancient barbaric tribes of old,
Their clans lone care avowed.
The rending through of right cannot
Bring goodness when walls are allowed.

Imprisoned by impenetrable stone
They thought would set them free.
Instead, facades of brick and rock
Extinguishes my liberty.

They built a wall to keep others out.
But now new perils rise.
For walls not only keeps them out,
A wall ascends up on both sides.

2019

# Gold

Truth can be painted over with layers of cheap paint,
Inundated till in disrepair.
It can be scorched and burned with implacable fire
And may gasp in unbreathable air.

Truth's a lighthouse, the haven poor sailors have sought.
Truth's a mooring so gladly received.
It's a gift thought destroyed, but each ounce, when restored,
Is like gold cast away, then retrieved.

So no matter the lies, truth remains, though disguised
By pretenders who scoff her good name.
But with nothing to prove, truth arises unscathed
And, like gold tried with fire, doesn't change.

2019

# Truth

When the answer is yes, truth resounds with more yeses
That cannot be mistaken for maybes or nos.
But with endless attempts to dispose truth's resolve,
Lies connivingly strive against what truth confesses.

Truth's a seed deeply sown; it's an anchor's firm cable,
Bearing fruit that stands ridged, unshaken and strong.
No deception can change even one featherweight.
When invited, truth comes as a guest to your table.

2019

But the devil will gladly and happily steal from your plate, taking freedom and truth away from us and into garbage piles. We can and must escape the devil and gain freedom from him. We have been given the freedom to choose—freedom from Satan or freedom from God.

# Malnourished

My soul's like any soul you'll meet.
I struggle long and hard to keep
From things I loathe and most detest
But stopping by my table oft.
Though uninvited, there it sits.
A visitor come every day
And, in my wholesome meal, delight
As if it were its own, not mine.
With one intent: to gobble down
Each unattended morsel found.

Appearing brave, but be assured,
The portion so abruptly claimed
Is taken back when slightly stirred.
(What little courage was attained)
For once entrenched, I must repeat.
This brash imposter runs away
To wallow in discarded trash
Without a single bite to eat.

2019

# Where Is Thy Sting?

*(1 Corinthians 15:55)*

Came nigh the horseman on his horse
With weapons in his hand.
In spite of what all others feared,
This one would him withstand.

That horseman walked oft traveled paths,
The chill of autumn's eve.
Endeavored he to take with him
Those whom his vultures cleaved.

Mourn every soul this horseman stings.
But he was not of them.
The awful curse…the dreadfulness
Can never swallow him.

The grasp supposed latched tight is loosed;
That cup despised, o'er turned.
No fear could come to such a one
Nor hinder what he yearned.

For there's a shield held taunt against
This raging beast. Instead
Of coming forth in trembling fear,
From him the horseman fled.

2012

# As Driven Snow

I looked within one snowy eve
And thought how I was made of me.
How God formed us as flakes of snow
That seem alike, yet none the same.
A-dashing 'bout, each called by name.

He placed me on the winds of earth.
He formed and gave my spirit birth.
Yet choose I every breeze to catch
And choose my residence of home.
For I am me…but not alone.

The grubstake I have worked and tilled
And honed to fit my wish and will
Is gathered up from what I've found
And built of things I designate.
For I'm its form and architect.

Now I proceed to such its end.
Dare not I say he fixed my paths
Nor sent me on unchosen ways.
For as the wintry flakes thus blow
God made me free as driven snow.

Circa 1977

# Chapter 9

## Nature

For our first two years of marriage, we lived in the little town of Leachville, Arkansas. It is located in flat Mississippi River Delta land. Then God blessed us, and we were able to move to Southeast Kentucky, abounding in natural beauty. This chapter is only about our beautiful natural earth and all the wonders surrounding her. I trust you will enjoy the readings and that you always have or else soon will also enjoy the many beauties of our planet. There's no other place on earth like it.

## *Umbrella*

The burst of umbrellas bloom
So suddenly the sidewalks fill.
Exactly like the flowers do
When rains her hidden seeds reveal.

Yet just as fast those rains subside,
The streets return to gray again.
And thirsty sand, lapped almost dry,
Take back where flowers once had been.

2019

# Not Far from Home but Far Away

I've found this place I often go.
Not far from home but far away.
Seems I must be the only one
To travel here 'fore day is done,
Along this softly trodden road.

On tippy-toes the morning durst
Blend well with wakenings of day.
A honeycomb most pleasant drifts
To magnify these simple gifts…
Like petals fast asleep unfold.

Here time becomes my welcomed friend
Who passes by in slow parade.
So when we take our evening strolls,
I pause 'longside where'er he goes.
Then ask if I perhaps could stay

To watch some other magic bloom
Or stash away more memories.
But paths now fade; the moon ascends.
And I must bid farewell these friends
Not far from home but far away.

2019

# Falls at the Cumberland

Cumberland, Cumberland, anciently tumbling.
How far have you traveled?
How long did it take?
You must imperceptibly move as the stars do,
Apparently sleeping but actually awake.

Your journey by inches has formed cliffs and trenches.
Since well before tribesmen, your course has been laid.
Unthinkably patient, you've whittled out wonders
That centuries can't hide nor your handiwork fade.

Though the arctic winds dance, nothing stops her advance,
Traversing escarpments, dissolving their heights.
For the Cumberland, tumbling, models and shapes
Till conforms to her wishes, designing delights.

Aged river, this Cumberland, etched in old books
Or in primitive stone only eons transpose.
Whether past years, or present, or years coming hence,
With the skills of your sculpturing, wonders arose.

2016

# On Being Nature

I'm taken captive by this woodland.
The chamber walls are cliffs and rocks.
My food is fruit hung ripe and low.
No chains impede my midday walks.

My comrades...squirrels, deer, and foxes.
My confidants are always near.
I've yet to see one subject flee.
But relish in the magic here.

My captors are the winds of summer.
The timberland, spellbinding bars.
Ten thousand fireflies in the glade
Turn off and on like tiny stars.

The trumpeter swims right beside me.
On osprey's wings I sometimes soar.
In whispers I repeat its charm
To keep it absolutely pure.

For I've become the voice of tundra,
Of fallen snow and waking spring.
I pick my way through swamps and creeks,
Neglecting naught nor anything.

The mountain air, I breathe it deeply.
My hideaway's a waterfall.
For I'm the captor; I'm the woods.
I am the wind, the trees, and all.

(Original written 1980)

2016

# Tsunami

Coming darkness brought the predator,
Walking places he had never walked before.
Taking all, that serpent's tongue, a robber and a thief,
A fierce intruder seeking all who came too near.
Why harm so many small and weak and undefended?
Do your wishes so desire?
Do you love or loathe this harvest that you render?
What brought you from your lair?
None will ever trust you now as they trusted you before.
No passage rights were given.
And yet you came, though uninvited, still you came.

Perhaps you meant no harm
(The leopard feasts in innocence and unashamed)
Perhaps your strength also seemed innocent to you.
Unaware, the mighty hand you raised or were about to do.
In the depths of silent thunder, you were formed
Magically from what already lay.
Made invisibly, you moved against your kin but brought no ill.
Your fury was the resting lion, asleep but ever keen.

You rode the crest with talons sheathed,
A stalking shadow in the hiding grass.
But when the prey stood forth, you rose, you and all your sisters.
Alert and taunt, your presence grew,
Devouring any who opposed,
Sparing none.
Your teeth sank deep (you menace of the Nile)
Then disappeared. And they, as if you'd never come.

Who brought you from your lair?
Do you delight or mourn for those you take?
Are you the leopard feasting unashamed
Or pleasures find in your consuming plague?

"One night I came. I simply came.
I had to be…just as you are you. I'm me.
I meant no harm.
I couldn't choose the way I came, if gentle
breeze or threatening cloud
But came the only way I could… I had no voice in why or how.

Awakening from slumbering, I moved unseen
Until my wings took strength upon the shore.
How could I know their mighty force untamed?
I meant no harm… I simply came."

2005

# Quiescence of the Snow

Many perish from their swarming of the morning sky.
But the onslaught gathers more;
And the casualties are soon replaced
With spanglings voluminous,
Occupying every nook.
Intensifying over land, they overtook.
Tiny soldiers unrelenting sound the charge
And fearlessly advance on every front.
Be it small or be it large
Until subduing all and everything encountered as they go.
A bustling world silent stills
Beneath the hushing, soothing hand of a newly fallen snow.

2007

# Hungry Hawk

A redtail rushed my window sash.
I thought it strange that he'd pretend
To weave and bob with talons lash
Against what only seemed the wind.

But soon I learned the reason why
He scampered as some agile cat.
The nimble prey before him fly,
So he became an acrobat.

2015

# Insignificant Earth?

I spotted me a star today.
(Or actually last night)
Of all the countless numbers there,
It somehow caught my sight.

I asked if he had much to do,
Just hoping for a chat,
To talk the lonely night away,
Discussing this and that.

We've not much time to spare, my friend.
For darkness falls away,
And I'll lose sight and sound of you.
Soon comes again my day.

That matters not at all, he said.
I shine for all to see.
I'm such a star of magnitude.
The brightest one, that's me.

You're just so insignificant.
So quickly I'd consume.
Besides, I can't see through these miles
Your microscopic plume.

So when the darkness comes again,
I'll diligently search
But never chance to find you, for
Invisibly you perch.

Try puffing up that tiny globe.
Try shining…just like me.
If not, those meager things you do,
You'll do invisibly.

Invisible…perhaps, but you've
Mismeasured what's true worth.
You roam out there, alone and cold…
I live on planet Earth.

*In the universe, our planet is just a microscopic dot. But it's home.*
*Being little doesn't make you small.*

2014

# When the Mountain Danced

A single snowflake gently fell
Atop the ridge without a sound.
Though teeming, millions also came.
Tenaciously he held his ground.

As those afore and after pledged
To interweave their blanket cast,
Creating mounds of ice and snow
That quickly closed the frozen pass.

Through arduous days, his post was kept
That he not bid nor orchestrate
The mountain's voice and strength unleash
And cause its slumbering to wake.

Allegiance sought no hiding place.
This loyal soldier's bravery welled
That purchased rock and ledge retained.
Till unannounced, his foothold failed.

He tried to hold but slightly slipped,
Awakening the mountain's dance.
Then all the others followed him
In one tremendous avalanche.

2012

# My Fireplace Rug

Busy squirrel scampering 'bout,
Your home must soon be found.
For wintery winds may come tonight
To test your shanty's coziness
If it be warm and sound.

You must suspect, the same as me,
(For I can sense the cold)
That bitter wind from distant hills
Is coming down with sculpting hand
To us his chill unfold.

You've gathered acorns since the dawn.
Your stash I'm sure's complete.
But have you sealed the northward door,
Secured each lock and latchstring if
By chance this stranger meet?

For now, the wind has picked a bit.
Snow falling greets the eve.
My cabin door invites come in.
So I must hurry lest the path
Be covered 'fore I leave.

Thick quilts and blankets stored since spring,
Lie cluttering about.
Seem anxious for my shivering call,
As if they knew was something that
I couldn't do without.

You also must your lodge attend
And curl up, all snug.
I trust you stay as warm as me
As I lie down to rest awhile
Upon my fireplace rug.

2011

## *Echo*

I just said hello to my talkative friend.
He answered right back with a hello again.
And the more we conversed, he, each syllable, tried
To dress up and adorn from the valleys far side.

When I laughed, he laughed with me.
When I sang, he sang too
Until evening was settled and spread.
He'd accompanied all night had I chosen to stay.
He'd have matched word for word what I said.
But the homeward path called
As the sable cloak fell,
And my talkative friend, lost for words, went away.

2006

# Lazy River, Late at Night I Came

Silent canoe, taking me through sedated night,
Do you even know how far I'd crept?
Clever foxes failed to hear my coming.
Fishes took a startle as I glided over
Where, unknowingly, they slept.

The midnight's darkness thought he'd hidden things quite well.
After all, this cloak upon my shoulders
Certainly has made it hard to navigate this stream.
So I just let the breeze assist my going
As I tiptoe through his kingdom,
Taking care not to offend him.
For I am just a visitor from time to time, you see.

I've come quite unannounced to watch your goings-on.
Everything is satisfying, pleasing.
Toads and crickets play in concert.
The sleeping frost must stay his hand that test the land for freezing.
Quietness, your trusted ally, slowly hunkers down.
And dancing fireflies keep on dancing gracefully and nimble
Until I've little else to do but count the stars
Or watch a ripple shred the moon, then quickly reassemble.

The darkness never knew my name
Nor guessed what path I'd taken.
I was the silent flight of owls,
The peering down of secret eyes camouflaged in trees.
So now we watch, both he and I.
For late one night I came to see this sentinel replaced
By daylight's craft and artistry that begs the stream to waken.

2007

# An Early Spring Snow

Please pardon, ma'am, a snowstorm's brewing.
So shall I take these lampposts in?
I haven't time to douse their glowing
Nor stow your other outside things.

While walking through your fledgling garden,
Not yet acquainted with the cold,
I fear when soon the snowflakes dazzle,
The blossoms bloomed might wilt and fold.

Allow me please your seedlings cover.
They'd so deplore the promised storm.
And flowers, 'fore they wake to shivering,
I'll bring inside your homestead warm.

Come eve all places will be painted
By robbers huddled at your door.
I'd gladly sweep your cottage entry,
Else soon these villains take the more.

"Oh no," she said, "I love this stewing."
I shan't be stashing things today.
But watch them dress in brand-new clothing
Till even lampposts hide away.

2007

# Fire

A hungry flame pants forth her life.
A vortex lodging shameless fire.
Her only thought is to survive
Upon the prey sustaining her.

A piracy who sinks the ship.
A thief who steals but nothing keeps.
A novel scribed in blowing sand,
Forever lost in desert deeps.

And so is she, this feasting fire.
The spreading plague to her has swarmed.
That raging life now finally rests
Amid the ash her very finger formed.

Circa 1983

# Secret Camp

In distant woods, my steps lay down
As winter's snow sets in.
No trails come round, nor pathways meet
To trace the way I've been.

'Neath frozen cliffs, my campfire speaks,
Entangling ice and trees.
No other souls have likely seen
This secret camp...nor me.

The river learns new languages,
A course her fingers comb.
Unheard, the night wings in; I know
More stars come here than home.

I'm surely first to walk this place,
This forest spared of man.
Tonight I'll camp still deeper in
This untouched hidden land.

1982

# Your Tiny Steps Aren't Quick Enough

Baby turtle, born of land,
Your mommy left you in the sand.
A leathery shell protected then,
But who'll go with you to the sea?

Your ally's darkness…not the day.
For nightfall hides your passageway.
You should have left before the dawn.
Now frigates seek you. Hurry! Run!

Not many reach the pounding surf.
Their footprints vanish in the sand.
And though that tiny heart compels,
Few ever join the fish and whales.

Run, turtle. Run now…run and hide.
You have no friends to call upon.
That fragile shell and flipper fin
Must keep you safely. Swim now. Swim!

1982

# Gathering Wood for a Winter's Night Stay

On mountain sides that seldom feel a footprint lay,
Where trees stretch out to trails unknown.
I've gathered in wood for a winter's night stay
Since eve had much to do
Before the coming night was grown.

A snow stopped by to peep inside my window sash.
I'd best leave soon…the narrow path no promise makes.
My sleigh may never know how precious be this wooden cache
As evening falls asleep,
And night, its circling complete, awakes.

The village lights far down the hill burn faint and gray
From snows exploring everywhere.
But I've gathered wood for this winter's night stay,
And these cabin walls are warm
Inside my cozy mountain lair.

1981

# Invaders Came Again Last Night

Invaders came again last night,
Their forms opaque,
Their feet unstill
And moved upon vast miles of earth
They'd captured for a while.

But morning broke as sunbeams woke
To spot them with their prey.
Each feasting on a hidden land,
Exploring every valley found
Until the dawn the night outran.

Now each invader stretches forth,
Escaping from the day.
For fog that once encamped this land
(With carpentry that seamen fear)
Make clouds their hideaway.

Circa 1978

# Chapter 10

## Scruples

Scruples: a moral consideration or standard that acts to restrain certain actions, a feeling of doubt about what one ought to do, hesitation to do something.

Making wholesome, wise, and correct decisions can often become difficult. Showing concern might result in an unexpected expense. Handing out kindness could cost valuable time. But doing the right thing is always the right thing to do. Being nice is a nice way to be.

Evil always seems to take center stage. Godliness, doing what is good, is frowned upon by many. It rarely makes the news headlines. Yet kindness, goodness, love, and suchlike are virtues that maintain the high standards of humankind and separates us from the rest of God's creation. We are the firstfruits of God's creation *(James 1:18)*, and being firstfruits, we should strive harder and harder to be more like him.

Before anyone can do any good for anybody, they must first be given the chance for life itself. Taking another life when they have no voice in the matter is not the right action to take. Life is life, regardless of size.

# Silent Life, Wholly Life

Desperately in battles to survive,
A struggling comrade bravely fights alone.
Do any care what great despair he's known?
Their spoils proudly boast from victories past,
Content instead to cast one living with the dead.

His outcries, never heard. He cries!
His screams in silence screaming!
By size alone elected they his course.
Just as coming winter banished to some tropic lands,
We'll never see the fallen snow
Nor speak his name
Nor know the things he might have done or said.

1984

Humility is not something usually broadly recognized. It tends to get lost in the mix of hate, revenge, cruelty, and even in good things, like bravery, leadership, and dedication. Sugar sweetens a cake. Humility sweetens life.

# The Commonest Man

If I sit down with kings, 'tis of easy persuasion.
For no kingdom nor king shall the noble despise.
So I choose sitting elsewhere; my joy, my elation
Is to help one less stately…my solace there lies.

With these threads of compassion, of kindness, and caring,
Each sewn to fine clothing that kings could command,
I will never contemn the apparel one's wearing
But most humbly sit down with the commonest man.

2011

# Nickel, Penny, Dime

The nickel bragged about his size.
A penny reasoned 'bout the same,
Compared they to this teeny dime
And boasted they a nobler name.

Their lanterns lofted bright and high.
'Cause after all, this special breed
Made them the very fondest lot
Of all the rest one could concede.

"We're somewhat indispensable!"
They both exclaimed in self-appraise.
Imagining they were the best,
No help to others save or raised.

They strolled around as royalty.
If asked to serve, just turned away.
"We have much better things to do
Than linger here," they both would say.

But at the store, the goods were bought.
That tiny dime, not they, she chose
To pay for everything she got.
(Guess values not what they supposed.)

It isn't from the claims you make
Nor flaunting high above the crowd.
True worth comes from within…not size…
And value from a spirit bowed.

2014

Never quit! My dad wrote in his Bible he carried with him throughout World War II, "When a task is once begun, never leave it till it's done. Be the task great or small, do it well or not at all." Never quit! Especially when the going gets tough. When the going gets tough, the tough get going.

He wrote a note I found placed inside that Bible: "Baltimore—Texas—Louisiana—NY Harbor—England—France—Holland—Germany—Belgium—across the Atlantic Ocean—back to Clarksburg and back home to Arkansas. Carried this book through all the travel and have kept it through the years." Not only did he keep that Bible through the years, he kept the Bible's teachings throughout his entire life.

A piano can sit in silence for years, but it will still produce beautiful music again when called upon to be played. Give your best, never quit, and always be ready to help others.

## Standing with Champions

Try as hard as you can
To try hard as you can.
Such an effort reveals
Your true stature, my friend.
When a challenge steps forth
And you take on the task,
You may not win the prize…
You might finish dead last.
For not all victories won
Will on trophy shelves rest.
But you'll stand among champions
By giving your best.

2010

# Tenacity

I actually thought I could sing…
But I couldn't.
The tunes flew like bats from a cave.
My clutter strewn dancing crisscrossed where it shouldn't.
This danseur all comeliness stave.

These oils and brushes just couldn't make friends
With an unpainted canvas I'd found.
All my prowess refuted, intolerably poor,
So when finished…a comical clown.

Taking readers on magical ways,
I'd thought I could pen tantalizing, fine verse.
But know what?
When I read all the stories just written,
My words went from awful to worse.

So forgive me, my pencil.
Have patience, my brush.
And these unfitting hands please excuse.
I'll try hard to do better to ever improve.
But one thing is for certain…
To quit… I refuse!

2007

## The Piano

Locked within your strings and keys,
Unable to release the savor kept inside,
Your music finds no winds to ride upon,
No stars to prick the midnight skies.

Ten thousand songs lie sleeping in your wooden frame.
But no one can awaken them.
No one has learned just how.
As bullion stashed in distant island sand,
The unplayed serenades remain unplayed
And buried deep for now.

And so in silence sits,
The strings, untouched, reverberate in vain.
Without a melody to make the handiwork complete
It waits, as hidden seed, for rain.

2006

Kindnesses done for others automatically brings you inner joy. Notice how good you feel after helping someone—opening a door, letting someone go ahead of you, checking on a shut-in, or even doing bigger things like buying groceries for the homeless or paying someone's overdue rent. Sure, this makes them feel good, but it makes you feel better.

## Kindliness

There's nothing wrong with being nice.
Like icing on a cake,
It makes the ordinary shine
And shimmer in your plate.

Nor none can fault a kind reply,
Though angry words prevail.
For kindliness lays still the waves,
And calmly waters sail.

Lift high your lamp of kindliness
To shine right back on you.
For it in turn will multiply
Each kindly thing you do.

2008

# Given to the Bandit

There's this bandit I know
Who steals treasure and gold
But then gives it to somebody else.
Oh, it's not like he took
Things as common a crook
'Cause he stole from no one but himself.

He gave riches to poor,
And if asked, he gave more.
Fame and honor were nothing he craved.
Every deed went unsaid,
Sown in secret instead
Just to help those whom life had depraved.

For he realized all things
Were not his but the King's.
And that nothing was actually his own.
So he gave it away
Never asked they repay
Nor one moment of praises condoned.

For these gifts from his heart
Were where love had its start,
Which he gladly contributed them.
Every speck, every ounce,
Every little bit counts.
Then his King gave it right back to him.

2015

Even going outside and enjoying nature can, and likely will, cause you to feel good inside—that is, if nature is left pristine for others to enjoy.

# Footfalls

A tiny patch of wooded woods
Kept quietly to itself.
Had not the autumn leaves escaped,
I'd never seen such beauty draped
In folds of doubled wealth.

The briars and thorns as jousters came
Across my trekking leapt.
And nibbling at each step, I asked
If I may through these woodlands pass
To find their secret kept.

Young acrobatic squirrels fled
As though I'd harm somehow.
But not one inch their land distress.
I'd gather acorns for their nest
If entrance they'd allow.

Then morning stretched a bit to find
Intruders came last night.
A fog invading wakened day.
But sunshine woke with sunshine rays
And bade the prowler flight.

Erasing every footprint made
(If I had made just one).
The crumpled map that led me here
Was stashed away...so it appeared
That I had never come.

2008

Of course, some have no goodly scruples at all. Again, try your best to not be counted among them.

# Foul Language

Like streams that spring from spoken words,
Once said, each one goes quickly in it.
And where the churning waters merge,
No dredge, no filter can unblend it.

Watch carefully, then, each word composed.
Make sure it leaves your lips resplendent.
That every syllable exposed
Is pure, for you cannot rescind it.

2012

# Swallowed by the Night

(To any who would abandon their child)

At times we turn aside
The moon's adorning light.
It hangs on tips of fragile thread
That keeps it for the moment there
'Fore swallowed by the night.

These photographs lie still,
Inanimate and cold.
They stir within remembrance chords,
But none can laugh or speak a word.
Nor flowering, unfold.

Some doors forever close.
Time sown will not delay.
So nimble steps she left behind,
This ballerina's promenade
Now pirouettes away.

How foolish who deserts
A child, their very own.
For in a blink that child is grown,
And memories wished are never made
Nor joys now seeking, known.

2013

A daily examination of behavior should be made. Consider highly what others think of you. You will have to live your entire life with your reputation. When I was a kid, there was a Sunday school teacher who would often say, "It takes 30 years to build a reputation but only 30 minutes to destroy one." Don't concern yourself with material wealth. Instead, fashion your life, your soul so that heavenly treasures will be stacked up beside it.

## The Perception of Me

I perceive me as me;
That's my interpretation.
But as others see me,
I might then take exception.

So I look in the glass
Of my conscience and being.
To make certain the same
Is what others are seeing.

2015

# Respect

If respect could be bought with this money I've got,
Then I'd buy some, my cabinets fill.
But it can't be attained buying, selling for gain.
It's a gift you must polish or stain.

And respect can't be weaved once the spinning wheel stops.
On such spindles it dwindles till gone,
Nor can it be possessed with fine purple and gold.
Though some think that respect they there hold.

No, respect must be earned, never purchased or masked
With a face unbefittingly false.
It must never be flaunted nor put on display
But in secrecy hidden away.

As a wise man once said, "True respects a balloon,
Round and plump with the air we provide.
But the moment a prick of misdeed penetrates,
The respect built a lifetime...deflates."

2015

# Whittle

When whittled through, this tender wood
Reveals a solitary piece of art
To cherish or despise.
Your trusted knife must do the job;
No other tool's allowed.
So keep it sharp and by your side.
For every part is forthwith hewn exactly as desired.

Each artisan can carve but one.
Take care, precisely plan each cut.
Make sure it's silky smooth when done.
Make sure it stands erect
And that it isn't cracked or bent,
No scars or flaws left unattended.
Then polish it with scented cloths,
Drenched through with fragrant oil.
It must withstand both heat and snow,
So shelter it within your palm
And hold it tight 'gainst coming foes
That run 'long side where'er it goes.

Then when your sculpturing at last is done,
The saber sheathed one final time.
The artisan's design, unchangeable, must yield its final form.
And what's been whittled…good or bad.
Will walk with you…your sole companion
To be presented to the King,
Accepted by him…
Or abandoned.

2017

# The Fountain Kept

They tell of treasure easily found,
Not stashed upon some distant shore
Nor born of myth or fabled tale.
This treasure's scattered all around,
Behind…beside…before.

No locks or chains, no sentry seen
To hold such precious content fast.
Instead, where every fountain wells,
All harvesters that come can glean
From riches flowing past.

"This treasure can't be spent or sold,"
Sighed many who gazed in at it.
"We thought contained within this cache
Was vast stockpiles of jade and gold
To keep our storehouse fit."

Their vision veiled…the gift forsake.
"We seek gemstones and jewels," they said.
This fountain spring can't riches bring."
So they moved on to ne'er partake,
Consumed by greed instead.

So only few will recognize
This fountain's love…not jade…not gold.
Far greater wealth is henceforth stored.
For those who seek that grandest prize,
Eternal life unfolds.

2003

# *Chapter 11*

## Blessings

In many various ways, we receive blessings. From a simple drink of pure, clean water to a safe warm home, blessings abound. Never take blessings for granted or as something earned. They are, by the grace of God, an undeserved gift.

There was this Son of God, born humbly, lived humbly, served man, and, just before his death, went to a favorite place. He loved this place; and I'm convinced that if gardens could love back, Gethsemane truly loved him. Jesus is now our unfailing star, guiding us on our voyage upon the seas of life.

# The Gift

In a stable in a manger
Under God's star at rest,
He lies waiting to the coming day
For to give us his best.

In a garden in Gethsemane,
By his friends left…alone.
Now he's finished all his agony
To prepare us a home.

2007

# The Garden

## (Mark 14:32)

Hello, my name's Gethsemane.
This man called Jesus walked with me
Inside my garden's open gate.
He'd sometimes laugh…he'd sometimes cry.
Back then I knew no reason why,
Just that he'd come, often alone,
And talk to God on bended knee.

He'd stay at times till morning broke.
At others, languish 'neath his yoke
Whichever way I'd welcome him…
But then, betrayal's kiss was sold,
And warmth soon changed to bitterest cold.
The rest he'd sought this final day
Passed by instead, and evil woke.

It snatched away what's good, but why?
Instead of life, he chose to die.
I'm just a garden, one he loved.
I can't go where he forthwith goes.
But others can, for he arose
And wishes them to walk with him.
But if they won't. Dear Lord, may I?

2020

# *Christianity*

The wretchedness of hate expounds
Unmercifully, claiming
Its plague in scores; its curse abhors
The good that love is naming.

For God's own word... Christianity,
On branches low, lies waiting.
The hope of nations hinges on
Its fruit, ripe for the taking.

2018

# Refuge

Stars in God's endless sky number more than earth's sand,
Keeping watch through unwelcoming night.
Like a beacon unveiled,
Inexhaustibly shines
If kept safely away from the foulness of man.

With unerring direction, with measurements true,
It forewarns of the dangers unseen
That the seamen can trust,
Navigating the straits,
Though a tempest be lashing the delicate blue.

Sending sailors awash by its turbulence tossed,
Unprepared for the harrowing swells.
Even anchors of iron
Leaves them helpless adrift
Through an ocean untamed no lone soul ever crossed.

So seek God as your map. He's the wind at your back,
Giving storm weary vessels safe moor.
He's your harbor of rest.
He's the constant north star.
And to sailors who seek him, he's all things they lack.

2017

And when the thirst for righteousness comes, he will quench it with the Word of his might and love.

# The World Pants for Water

The world pants for water.
In barren lands depraved,
No more than just a little flows
To soothe their constant crave.

Parched deserts speak of rain as myth.
Forgotten lost streams run.
Their guise…a valley wet and lush.
Their truth…a torrid sun.

So deep the mighty hemlocks feed
On portions for the strong.
Too starved to claim their rightful share,
Those weaker struggle on.

Oh, they who lap but salt and sand
Or ocean surf consume.
How shall they, tell me, find escape
From this, a thirst of doom?

How shall the arrow bent fly true?
How gather wolves with sheep?
They haven't splashed in rushing springs
Nor found one cup to drink.

But waters here assuage my thirst
And fill to brim, although.
I cannot count the volume come
Nor calibrate such flow.

For round me run redundant streams
To drench good earth…or drink.
The crystalline abundant swells
That quenches every need.

So cherish overflowing cups.
Pray God these springs endure
And that all others seeking drink,
As I, find waters pure.

2007

Yes, true riches, true blessings are treasures stored inside. They are kept deep within your heart, where they can be neither bought nor sold but are measured with the yardstick called love.

# Riches

I find I'm somewhat very rich.
I count my blessings, not my cash.
For money can't this stream explore
Nor through these forested woodlands dash.

For memories come from different sorts.
A treasure chest can't stir a one.
Not from these crumpled banking notes
Nor mansion's built or precious stones.

But if it could somehow ignite
A single blessing, by itself,
'Twould only just a moment last
'Fore prancing off with someone else.

True wealth and fortunes can't be sold
Nor bartered at some merchant's store
But comes in barrels, jugs, and pails
Filled to the brim…and then, filled more.

Gold dust and such are here, then gone.
My treasure though, no sleuth can hide.
I keep these riches safe and sound,
Where priceless memories reside.

I sometimes take a few coins out
And listen to their treasured song.
But when I place them back inside,
My trove of wealth grows ever long.

No vault contains such jewels as these,
A treasure carefully stowed away.
No clever thief could steal or take.
For deep inside, my riches lay.

2015

# My Trusted Friend

Inconspicuous, a flower
Relegates its secret wealth
That bedazzles with the colors
Fitly spangled on itself.

Bursts of phosphorescent glowing
Bathes a land once filled with shade.
Maybe fate arranged such beauty,
Or perhaps, that's how they're made.

Either way, this fragrant flower
Overspreads the canyons depth
And, with sweet aroma, covers
Mountains' height and valleys' breath.

Stopping by without appointment,
Never asks repayment made.
Just by satisfying others
Decorates the tawny glade.

Its unprecedented beauty
Chases off things wretched too
And, like trusted faithful allies,
Stands on guard the whole night through.

So when next a bloom bedazzles,
I'll recall my trusted friend
Who, like flowers, fills my chamber
With an effervescent wind.

2016

# Being Nice Is a Nice Way to Be

Being nice is a nice way to be
Like a rainy day changing to sunbeams at eve.
Or those stones in your pocket turned out to be gold.
Or discovering that old tattered trinket you found
Is in fact a fine bracelet of diamonds you hold.

Being nice is like having some money ahead.
Not a lot…just enough to get what you had wished.
You go straight to the shop and come home with your prize…
Oh, you've gotten a present for Mommy instead.

Being nice is like cartoons instead of the news.
Or like waking to learn school is cancelled today.
Or how about finding that doll you misplaced.
Being nice is a blue sky that used to be gray.

Yes, it's nice being nice, never stopping to count
All the big favors done or the small ones left out.
Being nice is like that, never measurements made.
If it's little or big…that's the proper amount.

Now consider our Lord and our Savior, that he
Left his heaven with nothing to gain
As a merchant ship laden with crates full of love
Purchased gifts formed through anguish and pain.

Making men to become as becometh a child,
By this deed given mankind and me.
Bringing love, bringing peace and redemption, he taught
Being nice is a nice way to be.

2004

## Chapter 12

# Faithfulness to God

Faithfulness is so very necessary for a happy, satisfying, and successful life—faithful to your spouse, faithful to your children and friends, faithful to your commitments, but most importantly, faithful to God. Walking on that narrow path of faithfulness will allow your name to be written in a book known as the Book of Life. Step aboard and continue on that train of faithfulness to God.

There is actually a map to follow that leads to faithfulness—God's Word, the Bible. Even if it has been folded away and stored unused for years, take it out and follow the directions. It will lead to home no matter how long neglected.

# The Map

I've seen it by faint candlelight
But folded it away.
Its wrinkled page placed in a box
To view some other day.

For I have roads left yet to take.
That crumpled map could wait.
I knew by heart each journey sought
And how to navigate.

But miles and miles of traveling
Has worn my wearied soul
And left me on a dead-end street
With nowhere else to go.

I opened up that folded map.
Its hidden path revealed
That leads me to another place
Afore from me concealed.

A tired sojourning wanderer
With just one way ahead.
Abandoning those other paths,
This road refused, I tread.

2014

As you proceed to attain a ticket that leads to your approval by God, remember there's another passenger who will board right along with you.

But only you can decide what train to take. The other passenger will abide by your decisions and will share your same fate. Take care to care for this very special passenger because doing so will make you very special also.

# Secret Passenger

Departing on schedule, this fully packed train
From depots the wayfarers throng.
Their ticket and passage already arranged.
Unable to board through the gates on their own,
They depart without privilege or rank.

Some rejoice when invited.
Some will sit in despair.
Some will entertain strangers,
While others shun everyone there.
To the King some will bow in approval and praise.
Many joy in refusal of him.
But not one has a voice in deciding or choice,
Being bound to another their fate.

Like echoing voices resaying what's said,
Or oceans controlled by invisible shrouds,
In all matters, they follow wherever they're led,
Moving only to places their host has allowed.

Nor they choose or select,
Be it mountain or speck,
To contribute at all to things good or appalled,
Caught and carried along by a resolute wind
Never asked to accept or reject.

Such a passenger too is right there beside you.
One dependently faithful and loyally true.
Take good care of him, friend.
It's your soul deep within,
Replicating each thing that you do.

2012

# A Captain's Log

This captain's log I love to read
Though mingled through with pirate tales.
For many battles had been fought
To keep his ship 'neath opened sails.

On nightly raids came mutineers
To spoil treasures as they pleased.
The captain though would chase them out,
Lest they his precious cargo seized.

They'd blunder every unlatched chest,
The crippled ship completely shred.
And so the captain wisely chose
To anchor somewhere else instead.

Stained decks were washed and cabins cleaned.
The masks and rigging sparkled too.
The silken craft slipped through the waves,
Long with her dedicated crew.

Now made seaworthy once again,
Although the bellows round her raised.
Although the angry tempest screamed,
The tiny ship atop it blazed.

"For certain, mates, more battles loom.
The sea and wind are constant foes.
But now our craft can stand the test."
The captain wrote, "Where'er she goes."

2014

# Walking on the Narrow Pier

It stretches high above the sea
Where storms dare oft assault it.
The raging waves and winds abound.
So I stand firm these sturdy planks
And tightly grasp the wooden rails.
Then, resolute, I walk it.

While on this wharf, proceeding as
A fragile ballerina,
Each taken step is carefully placed.
The stormy surf I now contest.
Till rescued from all dangers, dwell
Within God's safe marina.

2019

# Shores

The fishes love this lovely sea.
They swim its waves though unaware
That dangers lie about in wait,
Enticing them to visit there.

Intruders come, and thieves pursue
Where pirate masks and flags appear.
Refuse those shores of reef and rock
That even daring seamen fear.

The pricking barbs of fishers' hooks
Contest this landing soon to keep.
Forbid that even one should be
Entangled with or ever meet.

Yet though a tranquil shore is sought,
Confronted oft the ocean's kiss.
For balanced twixt what's right and wrong,
One must choose one as do all fish.

Seafarers come of every kind
Set course upon a passageway.
To either wreck on shoal and reef
Or berth within God's peaceful bay.

2017

# My Cup

I've a cup that's a catcher of many good things.
If I lift it above the encumbering clouds,
If I stretch ever skyward with steady a hand,
Not an ounce will be spilled…not one drop disallowed.

But insatiable evils compete for my cup,
Vultures circling about on impervious wings.
Diabolical predators stalk through the night
To refill any spilled with despicable things.

And the scorpion's sting with his poison reclaims
Every cup left abandoned; he takes as his own.
Moving hither and fro each container so found
In an instant refills with the venom he's grown.

So should ever I stumble or sway just a bit
All those good things collected could surely splash out.
I must thus trim this vessel; its contents protect.
For my cup only fills with the things I allow.

2013

# Things

## (1 Timothy 6:7)

These possessions I've got...
Things unceasingly sought.
Things I write...things I want
Of delight or contrite
Will one day disappear.
I'll become as I came,
Not a ring, not a thing
Will I wear, will I bring.
For the King; when he comes
Will take back one by one,
Every tittle and trace
To reclaim for his own.

So look past this and that
(All is borrowed...not owned).
To those things yet unseen
Not to things you've been loaned.
Look to what is secure
Where each portion you store
Will replace all you've lost
But ten thousand times more.

2014

# The Ticket for This Train Is Free

*(Romans 9:15–21)*

The train pulled in the depot once again,
Just as it had a thousand, thousand times before.
I'd watch it leave on other days,
Each car filled to capacity.
But now, quite unexpectedly, it summoned me aboard
To fill a berth unfilled
Prepared, reserved for me.
So I obliged…and thus I rode.

"Your boarding pass will soon be asked," the train conductor said.
Each given out to everyone who to this depot came.
"But did you carry it aboard
Through all those narrow turnstile gates?
No one's allowed to dine or stay inside these cozy cars
Without that ticket given them.
I trust you have it in your bag
Or stuffed inside your pocket or your purse.
I trust you have it with you now…
*Do you, sir…do you?"*

Frantically I examined every crack and nook.
If there was any place it could have been, I looked,
Hoping to discover it had been there all the time
And not misplaced by some neglect or carelessness of mine.
However, as I feverishly searched, the ticket master made his round.
His silver punch clutched in his hand…
Abruptly he spoke out,

"It's time to see your ticket, sir.
(A ticket absolutely free)
So little does the engineer request,
Just that you bring your ticket here
Redeemable for one last trip,
A trip completely free.

But if you failed to keep yours safe
Or hidden in some other place,
Alas, I'm sorry. You must leave…
Another train awaits."

2013

# *Famous*

I may never accomplish or do quite enough
To be counted among all those great and famous.

It's those grandiose things done that sets them apart,
Like composing some novel or rending fine art.

Never mind that some do it for riches and gain.
Though exalted and honored, it's all done in vain.

So I guess it not best to be numbered with them,
For their fame will soon vanish, their masterpiece dim.

And what thought as immortal will crumble with age,
Be it sculpted from granite or scribed on a page.

There's a way though that takes one to fame evermore,
That no one disallows nor that time can destroy.

Just be faithful to God and his song ever sing
Till you enter in heaven with Jesus, your King.

Where ten thousands of angels in sudden rejoice,
Bring you safely to home…
Oh, and famous, of course.

2014

# Chapter 13

## Just a Little Humor

Without humor, stress can overtake a person. Of course, things will sometimes get that way even with humor. But humor is like an escape hatch on a submarine. When it gets serious enough, use your escape hatch. Even when situations are very intense, a little laughter can help. Remember the humor of Elijah in 1 Kings 18? Baal was a false god trying to do something simple, but of course, it couldn't. Elijah said in verse 27, "Cry aloud, for he is a god; either he is talking, or he is pursuing, or he is in a journey, or peradventure he sleepeth, and must be awaked."

So be a little like Elijah. Allow laughter to be a light, not a darkened room. It can serve as an antidote, as a cure for some of the most common illnesses—loneliness, depression, sadness, separation. Administer humor often; it's good for your health.

# Left-Handedness

There's this wrong side out badge I've been given to wear.
It allows me an entry though awkwardly laid.
The machines need retooling…the instruments changed.
Many things seem bent backward, befuddling made.

Engineers who design such as these should resign.
Even scissors become an impossible tool.
And those lopsided desks cause my elbow distress.
Looking just to one side when they make up a rule.

But I'll try to adapt to their bumbling intent.
Sing the choruses first, then, at last sing the verse.
I've tried hard to be kind and uncritically stay.
But good sirs, your designs go from worser to worst.

2007

# Ridiculous Absurdity

Ridiculous absurdity,
That I was once an ape...yes, me,
And that that ape came from some soup
That accidently here took root,
That life sprang from it so intense
A million species now exist.
And all abide as one machine
That never squeaks or must be cleaned.
Things so complex to understand
Were formed but by a mindless hand.

If flight for birds is so correct,
Then why am I still fastened down?
I'd like to fly... I lean that way.
So why can't I, but only they?
And what of natural selection?
Who plotted out each course to take?
A billion roads and intersections,
No mindless thing could navigate.
From just a speck, quite naturally,
A trillion, trillion stars expand.
Or could it be that when God spoke,
Creation blossomed from his hand!

So what seems easier to think,
That soup was wise and planned these things
Or that my God invented me
And everything I touch and see.

2013

# My Canoe Turned into a Catamaran

Even coming on board was quite the dilemma.
My tiny canoe would wobble and shake
And try to turn over with me right there in it,
Unable to battle the gentlest waves.

There must be some way to avoid my capsizing.
Realizing solutions weren't too far away.
Without stabilizing. there'd be no surviving.
My vessel would sink from these surges it braves.

With nothing to save my canoe from this danger,
Tempestuous winds drove me farther from land.
My craft would succumb to this resident stranger…
But then, from the depths one extended his hand.

This master shipbuilder taught how I should build it.
He fashioned and formed till my vessel was trimmed.
Each leak and malfunction he helped me to seal it.
Then changed my canoe to a catamaran.

2014

## Tough Love

The blowing snowflakes scratched my door,
Requesting that I let them in.
The cold outside kept them secure
Since it was minus five or ten.

They clattered on my window sash.
Through night sashayed they even more,
As if to say please let us pass
And enter through your cabin door.

I wouldn't mind them stopping here.
My fire could warm each one the same.
But there was something else to fear
'Fore stepping in beside my flame.

They'd grown accustomed to the cold
And for them all my heartstrings felt
But kept my doors and windows closed
'Cause if I'd let them in, they'd melt.

2014

## Prayer Speed

Is a prayer like an email that's slowly typed out
And each sentence and phrase tidied up 'fore you send?
Then God finally receives it and hears it, no doubt.
(But I hope I've no problems twixt *Lord* and *amen*.)

No, I think prayer's like cell phones as quick as a blink,
Where each plea and petition is throttled ahead
At a speed even faster than human minds think.
And that God hears each word even 'fore it gets said.

2014

# Ducks

These words I write, I write in spite
Of others writing things just right.
But I arrange them one by one
Until composed, the verse gets done.
Most wobble like ungainly ducks
That no one else would venture touch
Or even hug, much less embrace,
Nor find allegiance to their taste.

But I enjoy their constant quack.
Oh yes, these ducks are mine, in fact,
I somewhat like them being 'round
To fill my air with quacking sound.
But if you don't like them that much,
Remember, there are other ducks
That quack a serenade sublime.
So love your ducks, like I do mine.

2015

## Wishing

"Please help me, sir," an eagle asked.
"With claws this little, I can't grasp
Or even hold the smallest prey.
I wish them larger, if I may."

Then, sure enough, what asked was done.
His talons grew each day—just some
Till he could neither fly nor fish.
Be careful, eagle, what you wish!

2015

# Hoot

A hooting owl comes every eve,
Reminding me the good I count
That blessings fall, caressing night,
So he hoots out a day's amount.

He doesn't know I hear him though.
His calls ring through the woods unscathed.
But when each hoot addressed completes,
It goes into this chest I've saved.

As eve politely drifts away,
I can't keep count the hootings made.
That owl must hold a passel full
That shimmers in a hoot cascade.

Sometimes I fail to recognize
Those hoots are his and not some crow.
I group them tightly in a bunch
Lest from these woods the least ones go.

For hoots both big and rather small,
Collect as dew on diamond thread.
I can't ignore the tiniest ones,
For even they through woodlands spread.

But if I use them up somehow
And all those hootings heard are gone,
There'd quickly come another owl,
For blessings hoot a constant song.

2015

# The Creation of Me

God made us earth, then faith began
That tells creation lies with him.

He made it all with just his word,
Though some dispute it so occurred.

There must be some more natural way
To logically explain, they say.

It must have accidentally born.
(You mean like all these cities formed?)

Did they just rise on magic wind
Without a builder building them?

Or maybe all these ticking clocks
Were crafted by some thinking rocks.

Seems such conclusions must be made
If you deny God formed and laid

The structuring of life and breath,
For truly, there's no answer left.

God spoke and all things came to be,
For only God can make a me.

2017

## Frogs

A thousand frogs, not any less,
Decided it was time to croak.
They squawked nonstop. They thought it best
No one should sleep, though morning broke.

Spring's early days warmed up their pond.
Her flowers popped up far and near.
Ole winter's snow and ice was gone,
But now, forbid, these frogs are here.

2019

## Roman Numerals

Such ancient ways could not endure
Like problematic math, for sure.
For it was laid in great long rows
Before an answer was exposed.

They'd add an L then minus D.
In complex ways, you must agree.
For MCMXLVI
Is just 1946…
Goodbye.

MMXIX (2019)

# Ageing

I've passed the age of growing old.
Each day I just grow older.
And children I could once outrace
Surpass me, head and shoulder.

I used to work from dawn till dusk,
Then eagerly wait daybreak.
But resting more now than before,
It's very hard to just wake.

Perhaps I'll find my youthful stride
With all its prowess teeming.
Perhaps again I'll outrun kids…
Oh well, no harm in dreaming.

2019

## Caterpillar

"Pardon," said the caterpillar
To woodland grass and trees.
"I'll soon have something nice for you.
Be patient, and you'll see."

In rhapsody with passing time,
He stayed his treetop nest,
Then tapped his magical baton
And hurried off to dress

In fine new clothes, as he'd supposed,
Till from those swaddles freed.
With fluttering of silken wings,
He said, "Surprise...it's me!"

2019

## Jonah's Whale

Our sins are like ole Jonah's whale,
Unseen but swallows whole.
Far out at sea, tsunamis sleep,
On shore, take every soul.

It's like one fly that's shooed away,
While millions wait outside.
And sin is fog draped on a lake
Where hapless ships collide.

A snowflake seeming harmless falls,
Then blizzards take the day.
No one concerns the gentle wind
That blaze the cyclone's way.

Yes, sin can be a peaceful stream
Till rains to floods give rise.
So watch, my friend, on every hand.
Sin comes but comes disguised.

2020

# Chapter 14

## Jesus Our Savior

Here's the gift referred to often in these writings. You already know this gift—it's Jesus Christ. The one and only way salvation can be attained is through him.

Jesus actually chose to leave heaven, come down to this world, and rescue us from sin. He left his home so that we could have a home with him. Although we are unworthy, Jesus accepted his mission and rescued us.

# If Jesus Stayed Home

If God wasn't here,
You wouldn't be reading.
You wouldn't be breathing.
You'd not even be!

If God wasn't here,
All life would be silent.
All things once so vibrant
Would turn and be gone.
If God didn't visit,
All right would be wrong.

If Jesus stayed home,
We'd be lost in sorrow.
No hope for tomorrow.
No "Welcome, come in."

If Jesus stayed home,
We'd not have a king
Nor a kingdom…nor freedom.
(What misery we'd spend)
So thank you for coming…
Lord, thank you again.

2003

# Parable of the Stallion

His home expanded bounteous plains,
His gallop ever free.
Bedding down 'neath star-laced skies,
Each dawn belonged to pleasant things.

Not once was played the song of sadness,
Never from these pastures been.
Secure and comely kept his stable,
Contentment sketched on gentle wind.

But past these grasslands, wastelands threatened.
All there by such were thus consumed.
He could have stayed where meadows flourish,
Where rivers splash, warm breezes fall,
And left us to the deserts burning.
Instead, he rushed to rescue all.

He carried them to lush oasis.
No thought to his well-being bade
And brought life giving water to them
That quenched their thirsts, lest any fade.
Abandoned none to barren burnings,
He placed each high on shoulders strong.
They watched him climb the dunes, undaunted.
He's come to liberate…he's come.

And as the last was born from danger,
Wearily his footsteps fell.
This caring friend, oppressed of burden,
Laid he down to rest a while.
He saved us all…asked not a favor.
He saved us all…from wastelands freed.
He could have stayed where meadows flourish
'Neath star-laced skies and pleasant things
Hitherto unknown such kindness.
He could have stayed. Those rescued cried.
A one as he cannot be measured…
But then, that mighty stallion died.

2007

# Suppose

## (Hebrews 11:13–16)

Suppose, my friend, when you began
That heaven was your first abode.
Your time on earth came after that,
So you know what each kingdom holds.

'Twould be an easy choice to make
If asked to pick between the two.
No one would trade a single day
If they the gifts of heaven knew.

But Jesus did exactly that,
Foreknown the consequence it bore.
He walked away from heaven's bliss
That we might enter heaven's door.

2016

# God Visited

God visited in silentness.
O'er barren fields his blanket swept.
He didn't mind the little walk
To see the place each snowflake bowed.

It loosed the thistle thorns embrace.
It dressed the woods with silvery lace.
Just drinking in the beauty there
Was more than we should be allowed?

The creek's abraded shores restored,
And aspen lost to winter's wind
Rose through the forest, clothed again
With garments God himself designed.

Seems nothing more magnificent...
An ordinary day reshaped
To heal its wounds...its furrow's rent.
Each withe and wicker redefined.

Yes, God stopped by one marvelous day
And brought to life a hopeless land
That would have vanished into night
Had not he offered us his hand.

But he came here...right where we live.
He visited not once but twice.
The first...to build a wondrous earth.
The last...his son to sacrifice.

2005

# A Sparrow on the Ledge

*(Romans 5:6–9)*
*(Matthew 10:31)*

On the ledge sits a sparrow, assured of his doom.
For his wings cannot keep him in flight.
So he waits his demise in that ominous tomb,
Where he'll slip into permanent night.

He had fallen alone, and though seeking escape,
Not one soul dare his favor outpour
Because helping just one could affect their own fate.
And a sparrow's not worth dying for.

So it desperately clung to that narrowing cliff.
Every movement made pebbles give way.
Until high on the ridge just a sliver was left.
Very soon the whole mountainside may

Be absorbed by the sea and dissolved by great swells.
No defense or resistance he bore.
For the moment had come that the hungering gales
Took whatever they wanted and more.

But as hopelessness reigned and unspeakable things,
Came a rescuer right to his side.
Disregarding himself, he spread open his wings,
And the narrowing ledge became wide.

By a bridge that he built, lest the sparrow be cast
To the depths that no mortal could fill,
But the cost was so great. "Who would pay it?" they asked.
Then the rescuer answered, "I will."

2015

# First Fruits

*(Matthew 10:29–31)*
*(James 1:18)*

(This little tale you're 'bout read,
Some parts aren't true... I must concede.
But certain as truth's certainty,
The last verse changed us...as you'll see.)

It seems (this might be true...might not)
The other creatures that God wrought
Spoke unto him and one day asked,
"Why have you made man first, us last?

We haven't done those awful things
That war and hate and evil brings.
So please allow this plea we ask,
Make us come first and mankind last."

Then he replied and each one knew
That God had made them special too.
"I hear your plea. I hear your prayer.
Not one of you is from my care.

But I cannot mankind forsake
Nor from him souls created take.
And so this day my son I give
To die that they, through him, might live."

2012 (original circa 1978)

He can give life to everyone. But he didn't come the way everyone thought a king should come. An earthly king, Jesus certainly was not. A King with a kingdom lasting forever, Jesus certainly is.

# Is This Your King?

Is this your king, who never wore a golden crown?
Whose robes were rags?
Who made no war against his foes?
Who laid no earthly treasures down?
Is this your king?

His army marches out of step,
For children form its rank and file.
Their uniforms, unmatched and buttons lost.
Look as from refuse found,
But each is daily washed and cleaned.
Its savor sweet,
A fragrance scattered all around.

Is this your king,
Born royalty of sheep and stable straw,
Who offers not a single coin to make his kingdom strong?
His throne and scepter few descry
This king supposed, attended by poor beggars poor.
His chamber doors are opened and unlatched.
Who'd follow him?
Who'd make him king?
"Not I," they'd say… "Not I."

So clamored all from palace walls
Built of the crumbling sand about.
Would he be king,
This stone cast down?
This lowly carpenter. They'd shout.
Is not a king as we supposed...
Look at his staff! Look at his clothes!
Who'd make him king?
Who'd crown him lord?
Who'd stand with him?

Then, with a sword,
They pierced his side.
Is this your king, despised and cursed?
An emperor led as a lamb.
Who'd stand with him?
For look...he died!

"I shall," God said.
Then...he arose!
From death's cold chambers, he arose.
And as the morning star aglow,
His kingdom through the darkness gleams.
From lowly birth to heaven's gate,
This is God's Son...the King of kings.

2005

# *Bread*

## *(John 6:68)*

I've saved many a sailor from doom of the deeps,
Making promise to soldiers…each promise then keeps.
I'm a ship on the tempest, unsinkably strong.
I'm the bunker to enter when threatened with harm.

I've brought riches to paupers and health to the ill.
For those wandering deserts, a watering well.
I'm the sunrise, the south wind, oasis and shade.
No admission is charged, though. The price has been paid.

Gold will never be asked as a passage or fare.
For this banquet I've made with no others compare.
Simply come and partake…every hungry child fed.
I'm the word of God's voice; I'm his life-giving bread.

2015

# Carving Names

*(Revelation 3:5)*

Nearly 200 years have concededly knelt,
And my name also bowed with each winter's snow melt,
Like a dewdrop lapped up by the hot summer's sun
Or a bright lightning flash just as suddenly gone.
Even granite relents to the blitzkrieg of time,
Though they thought it would last
Twenty centuries…or past.
Of such script so engraved not a shadow remains,
And the few who come by wonder,
What was his name.

There's another place though, twixt forever and me,
Where each carefully hewn name is carved indelibly.
Once inscribed, neither wind nor the waves can erase.
Nor the eons erode, nor corruption will face.
The relentless assault of life's robbery will end.
For like stars of midday,
Time will vanish away.
And the etching inscribed looks the first day it came,
For the Lamb of our God,
He has written my name.

2016

Everyone comes up short of God's approval without Jesus. But with him, the chasm is bridged, and we can safely find the favor of God. Suppose you lived when Jesus walked here among us. Would you have chosen him? Would he have chosen you? And just think. Even today, he will choose us if we will only choose him.

# Would He Have Chosen Me?

*(Matthew 25:14–30)*

If I had walked when Jesus walked,
Would he have chosen me
To be a fisherman of men…
Or just a fish at sea?

Would I have held in reverence all
The words he taught and spoke
And shamelessly proclaimed their worth
To kings and common folk?

Would I have stood as those before
And held his name on high?
Or when in judgment, will he say,
"You didn't even try"?

2019

## My Uncomely Sins

I pray that I may overcome
My numerable shortcomings
By coming to my shepherd's fold.
No other outcome dare I crave.
As he has come, I'm coming.

Lest I become uncomeliness
My Savior chose his coming
And covered my uncomely sin.
And so unto his welcome arms,
I'm coming, Lord, I'm coming.

2019

# Jesus's Blood

Since it completely cleansed
Those awful sins of Saul,
Then it can truly wash away
The awful sins of all.

For he, with evil, came,
Then came the Lord to him.
And just like Paul, our Savior's blood
Redeems us…uncondemned.

2017

# Deleted

(Colossians 2:14)
(1 Corinthians 13:10)

This dysfunctional typewriter's old rusted keys
Would respond unconcerning, no matter the pleas.
But the moment an error or mishap assayed,
There was no way to fix it or wash it away.

Oh, with clever disguises, the blunders they'd hide.
Maybe white out a sentence unwittingly scribed.
Or type x's to veil what they'd done, but in vain.
Even try to start new...but no paper remained.

Still, despite their attempts, nothing ever was cured.
Every error and misspell was there, not obscured.
And the paper that started pristine and unblotched
Soon became an illegible bungling botch.

And no matter how often they'd try to retrace,
No one could 'cause that writer just wouldn't erase
Nor correct any errors the typist had made,
Recollecting each one on the paper it laid.

Then one day came another...it glistened and gleamed
And was many times better than anyone dreamed.
The entire appliance shone brilliantly bright.
With one special key added beyond all delight...

When a word was misspelled or just one letter flawed
Or a capital used when it should have been small,
Every error and fault could be sifted as wheat.
For each one was erased just by hitting Delete.

2014

The thief on Calvary gained paradise. Through obedience, we can gain heaven. Keep in mind any and all small seemingly insignificant deeds will be written in eternity.

# The Thief of Calvary

(The one who took the best advantage of
any opportunity ever offered)
*(Luke 23:39–43)*

I was this thief.
No honor drew nor bade.
From others stole to satisfy myself.
Now here I am upon this tree,
Exactly where I ought to be…
But he did nothing wrong.

In my despair
To him I humbly pled.
Remember me when'er your kingdom comes.
He promised paradise awaits.
Such glory be this robber's fate
That I, a thief, received.

No bitterness,
For he forgave us all.
He taught of God while I beheld him there.
As one condemned, he set me free.
In hopelessness he cared for me
With unfeigned love untold.

I'm now with him
Who suffered all for me.
My agony deserved, consumed by joy.
Suppose I'd never met him there.
Suppose I'd died in my despair.
But he…he made me whole.

2008

# The Little Fishing Boat

*(Matthew 25:33–46)*

The ocean took my craft;
It's trying now to swallow me.
Billows apprehend my failed escape.
Impossibly I struggle toward that distant shore,
A speck upon an ocean face.
Rescuers probably were never even sent
To brave these depths I've every reason to abhor.

But from amid the tossing froth,
A little fishing boat passed by.
That stood atop the highest swells,
And then he took me in, as if I were to him most dear,
More valuable than breezes chased away midmorning's fog.
The shipmates gathered 'round in welcoming
To celebrate those waters braved.
And somehow each and every unpretentious deed I'd done,
Rather large or small,
Was written in his log that all could see.

I haven't time to tell you more…
The captains summoned me to join him on the bridge.
They say that he remembers every deed, and yet
It is as if to him alone each deed was done.
He weighs them to the very ounce.
And even small ones blossom radiant within his hand
As priceless gems.
A beauty none can replicate,
Nor will this captain…
Stowing safely every treasure brought to him…
Forget.

2010

# His Word

Listen carefully to every breath,
To every syllable so elegantly dressed and shod.
Just lend your ear and open wide your shuttered heart,
And you will see the voice of God.

He speaks with silent tongue,
But everyone can hear.
And anyone can understand
If listening is done.

His residence may seem quite far away,
But actually, he lives right here.
Right close to each and every one
Who choose to hear his precious word
And with unchanging truth confide.

It resonates most clear.
His voice is easily seen.
He's documented everything we need to know
And sealed it with uncalculated love,
Infused with selfless sacrifice.
No living soul can understand
Nor comprehend its preciousness.
For he, alas, to give to us this sacred word
He died...
Indeed, he truly died.

2019

# The Carpenter

This cluttered house is all I've known
Though not composed of straw or stone.
I've tended it, but must confess
Sometimes I find it quite the mess.
For left undone are many things,
Like mending roofs before it rains
Or dirt about its halls unswept.
Some things I shouldn't keep... I've kept.

But still I gaze, admiring it,
Till realizing how unfit
And must on someone else rely
To fix these broken parts, not I.
For nails and hammers can't repair
This awful mess I've made in here.

I need a carpenter... I've heard
This one called Jesus gives his word
To wash my house and make it new
If only I allow him to
Replace those things I cannot change.
The scattered pieces rearrange.

As he had countless times before,
He gently knocked upon my door.
But this time I allowed him in,
And now my house is clean again.

2018

# In the Book of Life

### (Matthew 10:32)

I stood there waiting…waiting.
The consequence appalled
While contemplating what might be.
Has every name been called?

The Book of Life laid open.
All names with souls prepared
Are written down and hosts profess
Each one…but is mine there?

Did I proclaim him boldly?
Did honor I endow?
Was ever I ashamed to speak
His name…will he mine now?

I wait, anticipating.
My verdict apprehend.
Did I enough throughout my life,
This mighty one defend?

Did I hold him in honor,
Like fruits of sweet delights,
Profess him 'bout the earthly fields
And to the mountain heights?

Then from his throne he saw me
Before his glory bowed.
My worthless name he then confessed
And shouted it out loud.

2020

Jesus has given us access to water that springs up into everlasting life *(John 4:14)*. One day, each must trade in the life lived here for a new life. Make sure God will accept that trade in and replace it with a sparkling clean eternal soul.

# Water

## (John 4:14)

From an uncomely hill flowed a comely, clear stream
That could cure all diseases, make anyone clean.
It was there for the taking; come whoever may.
But the source, whence it sprung, was to vanish away.

So they poured some in bottles, this water so rare.
And when any thirsted, the water was there.
To the blind, sight was given; the lame again walked.
It could heal all disease…even silent tongues talked.

And somehow it could travel on breezes and winds,
Touching far away doorsteps to easily heal them.
Such a gift should be handled as delicate lace.
Not one thread of it perish nor chance it to waste.

But as strange as it seems, some despised and refused
To allow such a water to heal or be used.
So they broke every vessel and emptied each vial,
And, deciding they'd won, not one drop would allow.

Every vat was torn open and broken each glass.
Disregarding its healing, they shattered each flask.
So the blessings were lost; every teaching ignored.
Dare not heed they its claims nor the wonders outpoured.

How could any reject such a fount gushing forth
As some undesired clutter of valueless worth?
For its taste was sweet honey that instantly healed.
But instead of just drinking it, rather, they killed

This deliverer of good that we desperately yearn,
Yet the water splashed out and will never return.
But as each drop was spilled, it soaked deep in the earth
And healed us of our sins...that we not again thirst.

2014

# Trading Cars

I drove my old car to a busy car lot.
It was rusted and dented and just wouldn't do.
All the years were revealed as I went through the gate.
So I hoped to get maybe a dollar or two.

That worn-out forty-seven, a sad vagabond,
Looking more of a wreck than a car.
How will I ever manage to make the next town
Once this broken-down flivver is gone?

The owner politely requested my keys.
His mechanic then took it inside.
"Don't worry my friend. We'll give a good deal.
You won't have to negotiate here."

Not negotiate here? What could that mean?
For I've but this jalopy worth hardly a thing.
It burns too much oil, and the motor needs work.
Can't remember a time it would start on one try.
The transmission is bad, and it shimmies on turns...
Her top speed is about 25.

"I like this old car...you've taken good care.
Don't despair that the years show its aging.
I've inspected her bumper to bumper to find
That the outside and inside are whistling clean,
Despite all the hard journeys it's seen.
A mud-laden road could have buried it whole.
But you've kept her well-polished, and the windows are spotless.
I like this old car...and I like it a lot..."

Then he reached in his pocket and handed me keys.
"Here, these are yours. I'll trade with you," he said.
"No haggling…no dickering…no negotiating here.
Your old car for that new one waiting for you right there."

Ah, the shiny wheels glistened.
Not one thing was missing.
Not a flaw, not a scratch, everything on it matched.
(I must surely owe more than I'll ever be able to pay.)

"Are you pleased?" he inquired.
"We'll trade even, these cars.
For you've taken good care of this first one you owned."

"We'll trade even? But, sir, I must surely owe some?"
"Not a thing," he replied. "It's been paid, paid in full!"

I collapsed in the seat…overwhelmed…overcome
That a one such as he cared for one such as me.
And this transport now owned
Undeservedly so.
Unimaginably joy'd, I drove home.

2007

Finally, never deny but always profess and be faithful to Jesus Christ, the Word.

# His Name

*(Matthew 10:33)*
*(Matthew 25:41)*

When came this stranger to my door,
I wouldn't raise his name.
I'd blush if asked to stand with him…
He thought of me the same.

When others were denying him
As though they never knew,
I stood with them nor dared confess…
Then he denied me too.

2016

# Guide

This guide I have stands close beside
And suits me to a tee.
I trust him with my life...indeed,
He gave his life for me!

He doesn't ask much in return,
Just that I do my best.
And one day 'cross life's bar with him...
He'll handle all the rest.

2015

# That Is to Say...

## Chapter 1
## Time

2:27 AM—One minute of time but just another minute like all the others.

Along the Coursing Tide—Life is like an ocean wave, here for an instant, then gone.

Tick—There is no stopping time.

If I Could Stash Some Time Away—Controlling time would only bring disaster.

A Clockwork to Eternity—Our visit here on earth is just the very beginning of our stay in eternity.

Life—Life takes on various characteristics but always continues through good times and bad.

The Wizardry of Time—In youth, time moves slowly but grows faster and faster with age.

Leaving—Make the very best of days to come.

I Used to Be the Wind—In youth, I could run fast, but now, a mere crawl.

Aging's Irony—Sometime age prevents you doing the very things you couldn't do when young.

Quilters—Your works will follow you.

Perception—Maybe the perception of time is different for different animals.

Pillager—For those faithful, death is nothing to fear.

As the Train Passes By—Once the final train car passes by (life), you must follow (death).

## Chapter 2
## God Our Refuge

Faith—Although many things remain unexplained, faith can cover them all.

Promotion—Strive toward the greatest promotion of all: heaven.

If Ever There Were Friends Indeed—God is our true, faithful friend.

But He Didn't—God could have, but he didn't, forget us.

The Gift Shop—Serving Satan costs a lot; salvation is free.

Paper Bridge—With seemingly inadequate things to do the job, God does the job.

Unfaithful to the Serpent's Call—The devil really gets mad when you refuse his tempting call.

The Maid of Naaman—Just as Naaman's leprosy was cleansed, the faithful will be cleansed of sin.

Candle of Life—Through Christ, we can now access the candle of eternal life.

God—Sin will overtake unless you rely on God.

To Even Be Given the Least Part of Heaven—Just a tiny place in heaven will bring eternal joy.

## Chapter 3
## Caring for Earth

Turtle Shell—God created earth in simple elegance and protects it with invisible air.

Stony Brook—Nature may seem invincible, but it can easily be destroyed.

Pioneer—The careless destruction of nature.

Fragile Island Earth—If abused and neglected for too long, earth could fall.

What Pirates Haven't Found—Take care of nature.

Forests—Will earth's trees one day be as rare as snow leopards?

The Connoisseur of Doing Right—Three woodsmen see the perfect tree to take but instead leave it alone.

The Bread We Cast Away—Many have food to spare but cast scraps to ravens while children starve.

Mankind—The often total abuse of earth by man.

The Surrendering of Earth—Nature makes but small intrusions on mankind, although man will annihilate even the finest bits of nature that interferes with his ruthless assault.

Essentual as the Air I Breathe—Love and care for earth; it is our one and only outpost.

Concerning Earth—A delicious soup in a fragile cup, protect earth or it could be destroyed.

Isn't This Earth?—A polluted earth becomes unrecognizable.

## Chapter 4
### Man's Exploration

This Mighty Ship… Invincible?—The loss of *Titanic* thought unsinkable.

Voyager—NASA space probe *Voyager* destined for unknown places.

Apollo Forgotten—After centuries have passed, will Apollo moon landings even be remembered?

Galactic Gumballs—Space is enormous, and if God created life elsewhere, we can only look at its star.

STS—The last flight of the space shuttle.

Rider of the Flames—The loss of shuttle *Challenger*.

## Chapter 5
### Losing Loved Ones

Vanessa—Losing children, any child, is so very, very hard.

Flowers of a Different Kind—A beautiful life of wealth and luxury doesn't make beauty; it comes from within.

With Wings and Other Things—My wife now has nothing but happiness and freely moves about heaven.

Her Angels Sing in Heaven—Donna would often sing from room to room here, but now she sings in heaven.

Forgotten Decoration—My dad, a freedom fighter.

Two Butterflies—Two who never met, my mom and my grand-
daughter.
The Train to Albuquerque—My mom loved trains, and now her
train has left.
The Lilac Flowering—The call of a faithful servant into eternity.
The Settlement of Lauratown—"Laurietown" and my dad, one and
the same.
Two Diamonds—The loss of both parents.
Empty Canoe—Like so many others…forgotten.

Chapter 6
Life's Journey

The Township—Judgment (the town) is everyone's final destination.
It—Life is just a loan from God; use it wisely.
Cabin Home—You have a cabin (life), but then the landlord (God)
asks for it back.
Scat—Resist the devil, and he will flee.
Shattered Bottles—Evil will dominate unless completely cast out and
crushed.
My Alcoholic Friend—Uncontrolled anger…or losing your temper.
Mayo Kider—Be strengthened by every life experience.
A Ripple on the Pond—Life comes; life goes.
Stepping Up the Ladder's Rungs—Aging means climbing higher but
on an ever-weakening ladder.
Forever—Our special gift from God: eternal life.
You—Although seeming like millions of others, everyone is special
and unique.
Blue Marlin—Tiny fish (life) we all know, but blue marlin (eternity),
no one has seen.
Hiring—Work faithfully now so you can have a retirement in heaven.
The Great Circus Ball—Good things, bad things, try to accept them
all.

## Chapter 7
### Lies and Deception

Lies—A lie will come as sweet as fruit, then soon destroy.

Thunder—Lies spread rapidly, like thunder from a lightning flash.

Hyenas—Don't discriminate; everyone should be treated as equal.

I Just Want Christmas—The murder of innocent children is the most cowardly way of the coward.

Intruder at My Door—If allowed entry, the devil will do all he can to take all he can.

A Prince Refused—Satan is the prince of this world; but Jesus, our King, overcame him.

## Chapter 8
### Freedom and Truth

Tremendous Machine—Secretariat, running fast and free.

Even Gentle Wind—Freedom is a very fragile thing.

Forefathers—Through many battles and wars, good, dedicated people have fought for our freedom.

A Walk in Backwood Woods and Free—Never take freedom for granted; it can be lost.

Walls—Walls divide everything and everyone. The result: no one is free.

Truth—It never changes, and when accepted, truth becomes a best friend.

Gold—Absolutely nothing changes truth.

Malnourished—If sin receives no nutrition, it will soon starve.

Where Is Thy Sting?—With true trust in God, the fear of death is vanquished.

As Driven Snow—Although we have been created by God, we can still do as we please.

## Chapter 9
## Nature

Simply Nature—Like I said, there's no other place on earth like the beauty and magnificence of our natural world. Get out there and enjoy it.

## Chapter 10
## Scruples

Silent Life, Wholly Life—Who knows when the soul enters a baby? Abortion gives it no chance.

The Commonest Man—Everyone is equal.

Nickel, Penny, Dime—Thinking highly of yourself doesn't make you higher than anyone else.

Standing with Champions—Always give your best effort.

Tenacity—Never quit.

The Piano—An unplayed piano still has music inside. Don't hide away your talents.

Kindliness—Kindness breeds kindness.

Given to the Bandit—Those who do unselfish, good deeds will soon be repaid.

Footfalls—Visit nature without leaving a trace of that visit behind.

Foul Language—Keep your words pure; your mouth represents you.

Swallowed by the Night—When parents desert children, the outcome is irreparable.

The Perception of Me—Do others see me as I see me?

Respect—Your reputation and respect are fragile qualities built over a lifetime.

Whittle—Shape and form your life so God will accept it.

A Fountain Kept—Recognize the greater wealth.

Chapter 11
Blessings

The Gift—The story of Jesus in 45 words.

The Garden—Gethsemane loved Jesus and would gladly take a place in heaven with him.

Christianity—Hate fills the world. Christianity offers the fruits of peace.

Refuge—Depend upon God for a safe voyage through life.

The World Pants for Water—Blessings come in many different ways.

Riches—True riches are stored within your heart, not in your wallet.

My Trusted Friend—Friends, just like flowers, sweeten the whole world.

Being Nice Is a Nice Way to Be—Or the Golden Rule.


Chapter 12
Faithfulness to God

The Map—Keep your life pure.

Secret Passenger—We all live our own life but carry with us a soul that will reap everything we do.

A Captain's Log—The wise captain of your soul (you) will keep his ship (life) trimmed.

Walking on the Narrow Pier—Stay faithful to the narrow way of truth to reach safety.

Shores—Fish (us) must confront both safe and dangerous seas on life's journey.

My Cup—Fill your life with good, not evil.

Things—Don't concern yourself with temporary borrowed things but instead with things eternal.

The Ticket for This Train Is Free—A ticket (faithfulness) is required for salvation, or else another train waits.

Famous—To attain fame forever, serve God.

## Chapter 13
## Just a Little Humor

Left-handedness—"Righties" have made everything wrong.

Ridiculous Absurdity—The creator of all life is God, not some primeval soup.

My Canoe Turned into a Catamaran—God can stabilize even the most unstable.

Tough Love—Sometime it's hard not to do the wrong thing.

Prayer Speed—God knows even before we ask.

Ducks—Not everyone likes the same things.

Wishing—Often what we want and wish for is not good for us.

Hoot—Blessings come unnumbered.

The Creation of Me—There's no such thing as accidental life.

Frogs—Ribbit.

Roman Numerals—Our number system is so much easier than that of Rome.

Aging—There's no returning to youth.

Caterpillar—What a pleasant surprise, Mr. Butterfly.

Jonah's Whale—Sin comes unexpectedly, and then transforms.

## Chapter 14
## Jesus Our Savior

If Jesus Stayed Home—Jesus chose to come. Without him, we'd have no freedom from our sins.

Parable of the Stallion—He could have stayed in heaven, but instead, he suffered and died.

Suppose—Knowing his ultimate end, Jesus came to earth for us anyway.

God Visited—The Creator of life also created salvation for us through his Son.

A Sparrow on the Ledge—Although we are unworthy, Jesus rescued us.

First Fruits—Innocent nature yearns to be as high as man, so God made evil man righteous through Christ.

Is This Your King?—Though not as supposed by many, Jesus is indeed our King of kings.

Bread—God's Word, free to all, brings eternal life.

Carving Names—Names scribed on markers won't last; those scribed in heaven will endure forever.

Would He Have Chosen Me?—Am I a dedicated servant of God?

My Uncomely Sins—Coming to Jesus will result in overcoming sin.

Jesus's Blood—This blood can remove each and every sin.

Deleted—The old law could not remove sins; Christ's new law can.

The Thief of Calvary—This is what I call taking advantage of a situation.

The Little Fishing Boat—God will remember even the smallest good deeds.

His Word—God's Word can save our soul but require a high price be paid.

The Carpenter—Jesus can cleanse even the most wicked.

In the Book of Life—Stand faithful in Christ, and your name will be confessed by him.

Water—They killed the Great Physician, but in so doing, it healed man of his sins through obedience.

Trading Cars—At judgment, the faithful will trade in their lives for salvation.

His Name—If we deny him, he will deny us.

Guide—Remain faithful. Jesus will handle everything else.

# About the Author

At about the age of 14 or 15, Gary G. Scott wrote his first poem. It was titled "Two Roads" and, by anyone's standard, not very good. But his aunt Peggy, a schoolteacher, highly commended the effort and encouraged him to continue with it. A little encouragement can be a big help.

Having a strong Christian family base is so very important. His dad served overseas during World War II, and his mom served by helping build aircrafts. God brought his dad safely home after the war, but life became financially difficult and challenging. Despite hardships, he saw faith unwavering, and no church service was ever intentionally missed.

His very first true friends were made in high school. Paul and States remain loyal friends to this day. No drinking, no drugs, no cursing, no off-color jokes—wholesome friends allow wholesomeness to grow.

Gary was also blessed with a wonderful Christian wife. Donna suffered from several health issues, but her faith in God never failed. She went to be with him in 2016, leaving a void never to be filled. But his children and grandchildren are a joy that certainly helps fill that emptiness.

Now retired, Gary enjoys canoeing, photography, writing, hiking, and just being outside on God's good earth. He'd love to hear from you. Send your letters to 512 Park Hills Road, Corbin, Kentucky, 40701-2593.

CPSIA information can be obtained
at www.ICGtesting.com
Printed in the USA
LVHW030947170721
692931LV00002B/163